Word Therapy

The Word of God to the Rescue

Dorothy Kuehn

ISBN 979-8-89112-983-2 (Paperback)
ISBN 979-8-89112-984-9 (Digital)

Covenant Books
11661 Hwy 707
Murrells Inlet, SC 29576
www.covenantbooks.com

This book is dedicated to the Holy Spirit, my Helper.

But the Helper, the Holy Spirit, whom the Father will send in my name, He will teach you all things that I said to you. (John 14:26 NKJV)

CONTENTS

INTRODUCTION

What is word therapy? Simply put, it is a word or a scripture that is just what we need now. There are times when I would just be thinking about an issue, and a scripture would come to mind. It was often a scripture I had not thought about in a while but was perfect for the moment. As an intercessor for over forty years, God's Word came to the rescue as I brought people's needs before him. This book reflects God's love and his desire to be involved in our everyday life.

CHAPTER 1

In the Beginning

When thinking about the beginning of the universe, I am fascinated that God spoke light into the darkness, and light appeared. He did not stop there. He created animals, plants, oceans, Adam and Eve, everything. Words are the first sign of God's activity that we see in the Bible.

Did you know that Adam and Eve did not have a belly button? They were not born. They were created by God, so there was no umbilical cord. In the Garden of Eden, the serpent spoke to Eve. Did you notice that Eve was not surprised that the serpent could talk? She talked with the serpent. The serpent knew the importance of words and used them to his advantage.

"In the beginning was the Word, and the Word was with God, and the Word was God" (John 1:1 KJV). Here is how the Amplified version says it: "In the beginning [before all-time] was the Word (Christ), and the Word was with God, and the Word was God Himself." Then in John 1:14 (KJV), it describes more of the picture: "And the Word was made flesh, and dwelt among us, [and we beheld His glory, the glory as of the only begotten of the Father], full of grace and truth."

So we are shown how important the Word of God is. And we see that Jesus is the Word. The word of God is the blueprint for our life. Hebrews 4:12 (NLT) says, "For the word of God is alive and powerful. It is sharper than the sharpest two-edged sword, cutting between soul and spirit, between joint and marrow. It exposes our innermost thoughts and desires."

It makes sense, then, that when we encounter problems in this life, we need to go to the blueprint to find solutions to our problems. As Christians, we handle issues differently than those who do not believe in God. Second Corinthians 10:4 (NIV) says, "The weapons we fight with are not the weapons of the world. On the contrary, they have divine power to demolish strongholds." In Ephesians 6:14–18, we are shown what these weapons are. They are also called the armor of God. The first five are for defense, and the last two are for attack against the fiery arrows of the devil. In 2 Corinthians 10:4 (NLT), we see more about these weapons. "We use God's mighty weapons, not worldly weapons, to knock down the strongholds of human reasoning and to destroy false arguments."

God used words to create the world, according to Hebrews 11:3. He said what he wanted, and there it was! Jesus spoke to the storm and said, "Peace. Be still!" The storm obeyed him. Jesus came to earth as a man and showed us what we can do. How do I know that? As you read this book, you will see the answers.

It is comforting to see in Isaiah 40 that the grass withers and the flowers fade, but the word of God stands forever. We all need stability, and we know that no matter what, the word will always be here for us. In Psalm 119:105, we are told that God's word is a lamp to our feet and a light to our path. We need God's direction in our lives. We do not know what lies ahead of us, but God knows. We know only a small part about situations. He knows all the details. So, shouldn't we let him into our lives in a bigger way? We are his children, and he wants to help us.

There are those who say they do not read the Bible because it is too hard to understand. The Bible was not written to our brains. It was written to our spirit. We are three-part beings: spirit, soul, and body. God is spirit and connects to us in the spirit.

I had a new beginning at age sixty-one. After thirty-six years of marriage, I divorced my husband and started a new life. A close relationship with the Lord gave me the strength to start over. I looked forward to my new life. A strong prayer life kept me in the Lord's presence.

Faith is released by the words that we speak. Those words that God spoke were filled with faith. He fully expected his words to produce what he spoke. The Bible says that faith without works is dead. When we read something relating to a need we have or watch a sermon, thinking that it is good information, and then just walk away, doing nothing with it, that is nothing more than mental assent. We need to be doers of the word and not just hearers. Make a note of that information that really spoke to your heart, and then do it or pray for it, depending on what your need is. If you just like it and walk away from it, it will not produce anything for you (James 2:17; James 1:22).

CHAPTER 2

Frequencies

Everything has a frequency. Why? Because God made it that way.

I studied this subject at different times and found it intriguing. Some people call it vibrations, and others call it energy instead of frequencies. The credit for this belongs to God, not the universe. In Exodus 20:3, God says that we shall have no other gods before him.

Our personal frequency is our state of being. The higher the frequency, the happier and more productive we are. The highest frequency is love. The Bible says that God is love. Therefore, he has the highest frequency. Also, we are told many times in the Bible to love. It is possible to love without being a doormat for someone. For me, this was a hard lesson to learn. Part of love is taking care of ourselves. What makes us happy? A bubble bath, coffee with a friend, a new spice to try, a new Christmas ornament? For me, sometimes it's just ice cream on the way home from work or a new jigsaw puzzle.

Positive thoughts also help create a higher frequency. We can choose to change our thought patterns. Instead of being down in the dumps, we can turn that around. I will use myself as an example. I had many negative thoughts about my job. I decided to turn this around by saying positive things: "I am grateful that I have a job. At the right time, I will get a different job that is a better fit for me. I am a blessing to people while I am on this job." This change did make a difference. I needed an attitude adjustment.

We need to pay attention to our thoughts because they direct our lives. They do produce actions. Proverbs 4:23 tells us to guard our hearts because it determines the course of our life.

Spend more time with the positive people instead of the negative people. When I am around negative people, it makes me want to distance myself from them. It seems like a black, heavy cloud accompanies them, and that is not a good feeling, the feeling of a lower frequency.

Thanksgiving and gratefulness are precious to the Lord. These are mentioned many times throughout the Bible. A grateful heart helps us to be positive people, and positivity helps to make our day better. In Psalm 50:23, the Lord said that giving thanks is a sacrifice that truly honors him. Calling it a sacrifice shows us that we should give thanks even when it looks like things are falling apart. God does not always take us out of the storm, but he can give us stability during the storm.

Paul's life was full of persecution and unpleasant circumstances, but he lived a life of thankfulness.

David, who wrote many of the Psalms, had a beautiful relationship with the Lord. He had a grateful heart, and God called him a man after his own heart (1 Sam. 13:14). David grew up taking care of his father's sheep. That time of solitude drew him close to the Lord.

Praise and worship were also important activities in David's life. He learned this at a young age while tending his father's sheep and spent a lot of one-on-one time with God. These positive traits helped to keep him close to the Lord during times of distress. Praise and worship also contribute to raising our personal frequency. It takes our focus off ourselves and transfers it to God.

Be good to your body and give it healthy, wholesome food. Eating a junk food diet is not healthy for us and lowers our frequency.

A few years ago, I studied essential oils and their healing properties. God made the herbs and all the plants. Any benefits from these are from him. Essential oils are known to increase frequency. A church retreat I attended a couple of months ago offered several classes on the last day, and we could choose two. I chose healthy eating and making an aromatherapy bracelet. Some of the beads for the bracelet were lava, which is porous. An essential oil could be rubbed onto the lava beads. I accumulated several essential oils from my study, so I was very excited to have this bracelet. I used a variety of colors for the beads so it would go well with whatever I was wearing.

I had a day off work and visited a botanical store. I bought an herbal tea called roasted cacao, one that I had never heard of. This is one way of being good to my body and enjoying my day off!

CHAPTER 3

Impossible?

Has the word "impossible" ever trotted across your mind regarding an unsolvable problem? If we could fix it, we would not need God's help. And there are those who think that because they have had a disease for many years, they cannot be healed. Too much time has passed. The man at the pool of Bethesda had been sick for thirty-eight years. The woman with the issue of blood had been sick for twelve years. Healing came to both. (John 5:5; Mark 5:29) And there are times when people die, even though thousands of prayers went to heaven on their behalf. We do not know how all this works. We just know that we are called to pray, and we leave the rest to God.

Look what Jesus says about impossibility. "Jesus looked at them intently and said, 'Humanly speaking, it is impossible. But with God, everything is possible'" (Matthew 19:26 NLT). I like the song "Way Maker." God is the way maker. Where there is no way, he is the way. Whatever it is that we are facing, we need to get him involved. He wants a relationship with us. Sometimes, I just say, "Jesus, I need to talk with you about some things." And I pour my heart out to him, asking what he thinks about all this. Some people do this and get up as soon as they have finished speaking. But wait a while in the silence before him. Fellowship is two-way.

I saw this scripture one day and was reminded that my prayer requests and my own prayer needs were, humanly speaking, impossible. I have no problem praying for God to move in these matters, and scriptures to pray for these needs come to mind as I am praying. We are told in Isaiah 55:11 that God's word will not return empty. It will produce fruit.

For those who think prayer is a boring exercise, think about the times you have prayed and a scripture rose as you were praying that you had not thought about in a long time. That is the Holy Spirit bringing it before you so you can pray the word of God regarding that situation! That is not boring. That is exciting.

> Ask and keep on asking, and it will be given to you; seek and keep on seeking and you will find; knock and keep on knocking and the door will be opened to you. For everyone who keeps on asking receives, and he who keeps on seeking finds, and to him who keeps on knocking, it will be opened. (Matthew 7:7–8 AMP)

I love the amplified version of these verses. They encourage us to continue to ask, seek and knock. Do not worry about wearing God out with your prayers. You are his kid! God's response to our prayers is offered to all his children, so do not worry about not being good enough, et cetera. He is not a respecter of people, as we are told in Romans 2:11.

Have you ever noticed a bumble bee? Aerodynamically, it does not appear that the bumble bee should be able to fly. Its wings look too small to lift that fat little body off the ground. However, they do not care what humans think, and they fly anyway. In the natural world, its ability to fly looks impossible.

The parting of the Red Sea looked like an impossibility. God delivered his people from slavery in Egypt. Pharoah and his army were pursuing them. It looked like they were finished. But God told Moses to raise his staff and stretch out his hand over the sea to divide the water so the Israelites could walk over the sea on dry ground. They were not to be concerned about the Egyptians. God would take care of the Egyptians for them. The Israelites went safely across the sea. Pharoah and his army went into the sea. God caused the chariot wheels to come off and then closed the sea, drowning them. Not one pursuing God's people was left alive. God turned an impossible situation into a beautiful victory for his people.

In the book of Job, we see that Job is a very wealthy man with ten children. It says that he feared God and shunned evil. This part of the Bible calls him the greatest man among all the people of the East. God allowed Satan to test him, but Job did not know he was being tested.

Job's children were gathered for a party in the oldest brother's house, and a strong wind came up and caused the house to collapse, killing all his children. Shortly thereafter, Job lost his servants and his animals in other mishaps. Then he was struck with painful sores from the soles of his feet to the top of his head. Job never blamed God for his suffering. Job's wife was not much support for him. She asked him if he was still holding on to his integrity and to curse God and die. His reply to her was amazing. He asked her if they should only accept good from God and not trouble. He was not aware that this trouble was not from God.

The Lord delivered Job out of this trouble and made him prosperous again. He gave him double what he lost. The Lord blessed the latter part of his life more than the first. What looked like an impossibility in Job's life was turned around, and God's blessings were showered upon him.

Jesus can make the impossible possible. He turned water into wine at the wedding in Cana. This account is in the second chapter of John. The headwaiter tasted it and remarked that it was not only wine, but it was also the best wine.

At the pool of Bethesda, Jesus saw a man who had been disabled for thirty-eight years. We know in the natural that a person who has been disabled that long cannot get up and immediately start walking. But Jesus healed him, and the man got up and walked with no problem. This account is in the fifth chapter of John.

The next time we see something we have been praying for as impossible, invite Jesus into the matter. Jeremiah 32:27 (NIV) says, "I am the Lord, the God of all mankind. Is anything too hard for me?"

CHAPTER 4

Speak What You Want, Not What You Have

In our blueprint for life, the Bible, we are shown that we can do this! The end of Romans 4:17 says that God calls into existence things that do not exist. In the first part of this scripture, we see that Abraham believed in God. Romans 4:21 says he was fully persuaded that God would do what he promised. It did not happen right away, but he and Sarah did have a son!

"And God said, let there be light: and there was light" (Gen. 1:3 KJV). In the sentence before this, we see that darkness was there. If God would have come upon the scene and said, "It sure is dark here," nothing would have changed. Darkness would remain. But he spoke into existence what he wanted. He wanted light, and that is what he said.

As I thought about this scripture, I saw the darkness in some circumstances of my own life. I needed to speak light into them and cause the circumstances to change. In the last part of Romans 4:17 (NKJV), it says that God calls those things which do not exist as though they did. This is like a reinforcement of the verse in Genesis 1.

As I started speaking light and life in my circumstances, I noticed that my attitude changed. I was no longer sad about the things going on because I now had hope. I knew that change was on the way. My actions were also pushing the devil's work out of my life. Look what James 4:7 (NLT) says, "So humble yourselves before God. Resist the devil, and he will flee from you." How do we resist the devil? We can resist him with the name of Jesus and the blood of Jesus. The name of Jesus is above every name, and it is above the devil's name. The blood of Jesus defeated the devil, and I like to continually remind him of this. So I say this, "Satan, I come against you in the name of Jesus. That name is above every name, and it is above your name. Go from me in the name of Jesus. Also, devil, look at the blood of Jesus. It defeated you! I hold the blood of Jesus against you! Go from me! I resist you, and the word of God says you will flee. I am a blood-bought child of God, and I am no longer your slave. Now go!"

When praying for the things you need, keep in mind that God is not El Cheapo. He is El Shaddai, which means more than enough, the all-sufficient One. Do not put a lid on your blessings. See him as the one who wants to bless you abundantly, not just give you enough to get by for the day. Do not be afraid to dream with God. Tell him your hopes and dreams. It is part of your relationship with him. Let him into the secret places in your life. He knows all about you anyway, but he wants an invitation.

When I was a new Christian, one of the first things the Lord taught me was not to put a lid on my blessings. I thought about what that meant and wondered what I was doing that was limiting my blessings. I was being specific in my prayers because I had learned that when you do not pray for anything specific, you will not get anything specific. But I was asking for a certain amount of money, for example, for certain bills, and not allowing myself to look beyond that. I should have ended the prayer by thanking God for being more than enough and going beyond what I prayed for, not limiting the blessing. I saw the fruit of that so many times. Our furnace broke at a time when we were not doing well financially. I still remember talking with the Lord as I went to bed. I said, "Lord, we do not have the money for a new furnace. I cast the care of our finances over onto you." I did not spread the word to my friends. I just told God. The next morning, we were given enough money for a new furnace.

There were fifty dollars left, which we used for groceries for the week. God is never late.

In the twenty-second chapter of Numbers, we see that Balak, king of Moab, tried to hire Balaam to curse God's people. The king said he knew that those he blesses are blessed, and those he curses are cursed. God told Balaam that he must not put a curse on those people because they are blessed. Notice that Balak sees the power of words and is willing to pay for this evil work. After refusing the first time, Balaam is encouraged a second time to curse God's people. He is promised to be well rewarded for this assignment. On the road to his assignment, his donkey sees an angel with a sword drawn blocking the road. The donkey kept stopping and was beaten three times. Finally, the donkey is given the power by God to speak, and she complains to Balaam about mistreating her. Like Eve, Balaam showed no surprise that an animal was speaking. I found this remarkably interesting, but nowhere else in the Bible are we shown that animals were speaking in those biblical times. After the donkey tries to reason with her master, God opens Balaam's eyes so he can see the angel blocking the road. The angel told Balaam he would have killed him if he tried to go through. Balaam repented and was instructed to go on to the assignment but to speak only what God directed. Balak kept telling Balaam to curse God's people, and every time, he blessed them instead as the Lord ordered.

We are snared by the words of our mouth, so it is important to speak the right words and not words that we will be sorry for later. Proverbs 6:2 (NIV) says that we have been trapped by what we have said, ensnared by the words of our mouth. This scripture is warning us about being surety for a friend. It is good advice in general because it reminds us of how important our words are. Also, in Proverbs 18:21, we are told that death and life are in the power of the tongue. We have all heard people who say their vehicle is a piece of junk and never runs right. Then they wonder why their car keeps breaking down. Others talk about how sick they are, catching every virus that comes to town. These people are speaking death to their circumstances. They are receiving the fruit of what they have said. They say they have talked that way all their life and probably will not change. Then neither will their circumstances. Just because they are used to talking that way, it does not make it right. If they want things to change, the first thing they need to do is change their words. Do not say what you have got. Speak what you want, but make sure it lines up with God's will. The word of God is his will.

I had been praying with a woman who was healed of cancer. Some of the symptoms had returned, and she was scheduled for testing. She kept referring to it as her cancer. I kept correcting her, saying it was not her cancer. I told her to quit embracing the disease that God did not give her. "It is not yours, and you do not want it. You can call it cancer, but do not call it to you. Listen to me as I pray for you. I will address it, but I will not give it any place in you." The day of testing came. A few days later, results were shared with her: no cancer!

Recently, I heard many people talk about allergies. They spoke about this subject, saying, "My allergies," et cetera. What they did not realize was that they were embracing this affliction. They were calling it to themselves. Angels hearken to the voice of God's word, according to Psalm 103. We all have access to angels, which were created to listen and respond to the word of God. But God's word was not spoken, asking for his help with this matter. So, the angels remained off duty.

In the eighth chapter of Matthew, a centurion's servant was ill, paralyzed, and in terrible suffering. The centurion came to Jesus and asked him for help. Jesus told him that he would come and heal the servant. The centurion surprised him by telling him to just speak the word, and his servant would be healed. In his line of work, he fully understood orders and had no problem believing that healing would be the result. Jesus marveled at this and said he had not seen anyone in Israel with such great faith. Jesus responded that it would be done as he believed. The servant was healed at that very hour. That centurion said what he wanted and had no doubt about the outcome.

Look at the words spoken by the woman with the issue of blood. She said that if she just touched the clothes of Jesus, she would be whole. She pressed through the crowd and touched his clothes, and she was instantly healed. In the fifth chapter of Mark, her story is told. She believed what she said, and she received the blessing. She was aware of her physical condition, but she did not say what she had. She said what she wanted.

Remember when Jesus spoke to the storm? What if he would have stood up and said, "That is the worst wind I have ever seen!" No, he did not say what he saw. He said, "Peace. Be still." The storm obeyed him. He was not operating as Jesus, the son of God. He was operating as a man. His disciples could have done the same thing. He asked them why they were so fearful and had no faith. Do I speak to storms that are coming to my territory? Yes, I do.

After the exodus from Egypt, the children of Israel kept grumbling and complaining to Moses. They also spoke about dying in the wilderness. They were snared by the words of their mouths, and they all died in the wilderness except for Joshua and Caleb, who brought back the good report, saying they could take the land. Matthew 12:34 tells us that the words we speak come from our hearts. Instead of staying grateful for their deliverance at the Red Sea, they quickly forgot how much God did for them. Instead of receiving the blessings God had for them, they died. Life would have been so much better for them if they would have cooperated with God. He gave them the Promised Land, and he would have helped them receive it, but they spoke against it, agreeing with the evil report of the ten instead of the positive report of the two, Joshua and Caleb.

The words we speak are especially important. We are shown the evidence of this in Proverbs 18:7 (NLT): "The mouths of fools are their ruin; they trap themselves with their lips."

Speak to the mountain.

In Mark 11:23, Jesus is talking about speaking to our problems. We have been given the authority to do this. As I looked at this scripture, I thought this could take a while because I had a mountain range and not just a mountain. These problems stand in the way of God's blessings and need to be removed. I made a list of the mountains and spoke to them.

This is basically what I said, "In the name of Jesus, I speak to the mountain of (a health issue) in my body. I command that (health issue) to be removed from my life and my body and cast into the sea, according to Mark 11:23. By faith, I call it removed, and I have no doubt in my mind that I am free from (health issue). Thank you, Jesus, that your word is fulfilled in my life today." If debt is the mountain, I replace the word, body, with finances.

Do not expect the mountain to move immediately. Be a battering ram and expect to see the fruit of your faith.

If you want to take it a step further, you can call life and health back into your body, according to Proverbs 18:21. This scripture says that death and life are in the power of the tongue. Romans 8:11 (NLT) says, "The Spirit of God, who raised Jesus from the dead, lives in you. And just as God raised Christ Jesus from the dead, he will give life to your mortal bodies by this same Spirit living within you." This is one of those scriptures that I wrote on a notepad to keep before me and meditate on it.

Why do we have all these problems? Because the devil is doing his job. Remember, he is the one who comes to kill, steal, and destroy, but Jesus is the one who came so we could have life and have it abundantly. When we get free from these problems, does that mean they will be gone forever? No. The devil is a deceiver. He will come to you with the thought that you really did not get free and try to put that symptom on you later. If you agree with him, you open the door for him to come back in and give you trouble. But you can speak to that symptom and say, "No, I was healed of you, and you're not coming back. Now leave!" That is faith in action. I have had to speak to those symptoms that tried to return many times, and they do leave. The devil wants people to agree with him and say, "Well, I thought I was healed, but I guess I wasn't." That is one way that people lose their healing (John 10:10).

Having a mountain range of trouble does not mean that you are a bad person or that you have done something wrong. Sometimes, people feel bad about their circumstances and wonder what they did to deserve all this. Jesus said that we will have trouble in this world (John 16:33). It may at times be the reaping of what we have sown, but often, it is just the devil doing what he does best.

CHAPTER 5

You Do Not Have Because You Do Not Ask

This scripture is from the fourth chapter of James. Some of us do not know what to ask. I was one of those people. I would take a scripture like this and just talk in depth to the Lord about it, hoping for more insight into the matter. I will share one of those discussions with you.

"Lord, I do not know what to ask, so I will describe it to you the best way I know how. What it looks like from my side is junk in my trunk, and I feel like my hopes and dreams are buried out there somewhere in an ash heap. I am not aware of what the junk is, but I want to be free. So, please help me to fulfill my destiny and get rid of what needs to go."

Now you may be wondering what junk was in my trunk. Because of the circumstances I encountered throughout my life, I had several things in my trunk. I had unforgiveness, bitterness, soul ties, soul wounds, and several things stuck in my cellular memory. In my second book, Progressive Healing, the last three items are talked about in detail. Although I had already dealt with unforgiveness and bitterness, there were still situations in my past that I had not thought about. As the Lord brought these memories before me, one at a time, he helped me pray through them.

God gives us choices. We can deal with the things that hinder us from having a great life that he wants us to have, or we can choose to let it go and move on. Some would say, "That was then, this is now. I just want to forget it and get on with my life." That is your choice. I knew I had some baggage, and I chose to get free of it.

What I did was part of what I taught in my first book, Get Real with God. He gave me the title of that book and showed me what to share. That book is about a relationship with God. When the Lord told me to get it published, I remember feeling like it needed to be bigger. The Lord responded to my thoughts and said the size of a book is not important. It is the content that is important.

Several years ago, I published three cookbooks for smaller households. A woman from Colorado wrote me a letter saying that my funnel cake recipe was worth the price of the whole cookbook. I feel the same way when I read a Christian book. If I get one golden nugget of help from that book, it is worth the price of that book. I do not read books to get a warm fuzzy feeling. I read them to see how God helps people in their situations. This often helps me in my own circumstances.

I was in my thirties when I became a Christian, so there was a lot of junk in my trunk. God is merciful, and he wants us to fulfill our destinies. But we must cooperate with him.

Does this mean we will get whatever we ask God for?

Motives are particularly important to God. Why do we want what we are asking for? Is it to fulfill our latest lust? That is a bad motive. Do we want to look successful because our neighbors look successful? Another bad motive. When we see another person's success, are we happy for them or envious of them? One of the Ten Commandments is "You shall not covet." Covet means to wish, long for, or crave something that belongs to someone else. When we hear about someone getting a blessing from God, rejoice with them, as Romans 12:15 encourages us to do.

Look what it says in James 4:3 (NLT): "And even when you ask, you don't get it because your motives are all wrong—you want only what will give you pleasure." If God gave us everything we asked for when we asked for it, we would be spoiled brats.

Make sure that what you are asking for lines up with the will of God. God's word is his will. Do you have a scripture to back up what you are asking for? Look at 1 John 5:14–15. We see that he hears us if we ask anything according to his will. And if we know that he hears us, we know that whatever we ask will be given to us.

Isaiah 53:5 tells us that by the stripes of Jesus, we are healed. He paid the price for us so we could be healed. In Psalm 35:27, we are shown that the Lord delights in the prosperity of his servant. Psalm 34:10 (NLT) says, "Even strong young lions sometimes go hungry, but those who trust in the Lord will lack no good thing."

I was thirty-four years old when I became a born-again Christian. Because of the strong desire to pray that came with that experience, I spent a lot of time asking questions of the Lord. I told him that he was welcome to talk with me any time, even if that meant waking me up in the middle of the night. I believe that is why my personal time with him is often in the middle of the night! Knowing that I had a lot of baggage in my life because of two failed marriages, I included a request along with my prayers that simply said, "Lord, I want to be free. Show me how to cooperate with you to get where I need to be." Unknowingly, I was asking for his help with my destiny.

Bitterness was one of the things shown to me. There are a lot of people who have not dealt with an old hurt. Before I came to the Lord, I really did not know how to deal with old hurts, so I pushed them aside and tried to move on with my life. As a new Christian, I learned about repentance and forgiveness. As I continued to remind the Lord that I wanted to be free, he continued to show me things that needed to change in my life. The Holy Spirit is so loving and gentle I wanted to spend more time with him, learning his ways and his thoughts. I remembered the scripture that said his ways are higher than ours, and his thoughts are higher than ours (Isaiah 55:8–9). My prayers were being answered, and freedom was coming, one session at a time.

Many times, I have wondered why evil people get away with the things they are doing. This verse gave me hope that God sees it all and he will make it right. Also, because I am a child of God, I am righteous and can pray this scripture. I was happy to find it. "For the eyes of the Lord are on the righteous, and his ears are open to their prayers, but the face of the Lord is against those who do evil" (1 Pet. 3:12 NKJV). I want to fulfill my destiny and am grateful for his help.

Sometimes, God answers our prayers in ways other than what we expected. We all have a destiny, a purpose on this earth. We see a little portion of what we want, but God sees the big picture. He wants to bless us, and he does bless us. I love to pray Romans 8:28 (NLT) when asking God for something because I want him to know up front that however he chooses to answer, I am okay with it. "And we know that God causes everything to work together for the good of those who love God and are called according to his purpose for them."

So if we do not get what we asked for when we think we need it, does that mean we will not get it? No. God is not on our timeline. We are on his timeline. He is never late. He does not think as we think. Look what it says in Isaiah 55:8 (NLT). This is so beautiful. "My thoughts are nothing like your thoughts," says the Lord. "And my ways are far beyond anything you could imagine." As we get a closer relationship with the Lord, we see how he thinks about matters that are important to us. Maybe that request for money will be answered with a better-paying job. For those who think God is boring, look at what he created: Instead of giving us one kind of bird, one kind of animal, and one kind of tree, he created so many varieties that we would have trouble counting them! He wants our life to be enjoyable.

Can we still trust him if it looks like our prayer was not answered? Of course. Proverbs 3:5–6 says, "Trust in the Lord with all your heart and lean not on your own understanding. In all your ways, acknowledge him, and he shall direct your paths." If you have asked for something that would harm you, he will not answer that prayer. A loving parent would not do something that would harm their child. Maybe he has something better for you than what you asked for. Do not give up, and do not quit asking just because the answer has not yet arrived. As I said in chapter 2, Matthew 7:7 is very encouraging as we bring our needs and desires before the Lord. We are encouraged to keep on asking, keep on seeking, and keep on knocking. Prayer is not just asking for something one time and then walking away. Remember Daniel and how he had to wait twenty-one days for the answer to his prayer? He was greatly loved by God, but the answer was delayed by a heavenly battle.

Sometimes people ask me, "God talks to you?" I am glad they ask because God wants to talk with all of us. He is my father, so yes, he talks to me. When I understood that being born again gave me a relationship with Jesus, I pressed in to build that relationship. Relationships are not a one-way street. How can you have a relationship with someone who does not talk with you?

The Lord has talked to many of you, and you did not know it. Remember when you often drove through yellow lights, and one time, you had a strong thought saying, "Stop at this one." Then a second later, you saw a car run a red light, and you knew you could have been involved in an accident. Another time, "something" was telling you to take a different route to work. You ignored it and encountered a detour you were not aware of and were late for work.

When I was learning to hear the Lord, he spoke to me with strong thoughts, like in the previous paragraph. Many times, he would include a word that I was not familiar with and have me look it up. This was one way I knew it was not just my thoughts. Sometimes, the thought was a request to pray for a person that I had not thought of in a long time. One day, I reached for a can of chili to use for chili dogs. As I was heating it, I heard to add a little cumin, and that would make it delicious. My first thought was, "Do I have cumin?" My second thought was, "He would not have told me to add something that was not in my cupboard!" I quickly found it. The chili dog was delicious.

I recently attended a class on healthy eating. The teacher said she uses herbs and spices liberally. They not only enhance a recipe, but they have properties that are good for our bodies. The day after the class, a flash from the past came to mind. I remembered the Lord telling me about adding the cumin to the chili. I wondered what properties cumin has for our bodies, so I looked it up on the internet. There were so many benefits I wanted to add cumin as often as possible.

God also speaks to us in his word. At times, the Holy Spirit brings back to our mind a scripture or Bible story that relates to something we are going through. This brings us peace, direction, and comfort, depending on what we need at the time. I have commented to the Lord that I had not thought of that scripture or story in an awfully long time, but it was just what I needed now.

Several people have said that we should not bother God with prayers that are not important. I am not in agreement with that because I am sure God is interested in the little things as well as the big things in our lives. He is our father, and our fathers are interested in what their children are doing. One day, Jim (my prayer partner at work) shared with me that he and his son were going deer hunting during the weekend. His son had never shot a deer and was hoping he would get his first deer this year. I said, "Well, let's pray about it." We prayed, and I knew there would be a smile on Jim's face on Monday. He could not wait until Monday to show me the answer to our prayer! He texted me a picture of his son with his first deer. His son's smile was priceless.

Several years ago, we bought a house in Iowa. After moving in, we found that we were not the only inhabitants. This house was overrun by mice. My first thought was, "Oh, God help us!" Overwhelmed and unsettled, I sought the Lord's help. Instead of leading me to the grocery store for mouse traps and poison, he led me to the local feed store. Feed store employees are familiar with varmints and how to eradicate them. I asked God for help and received help! The mouse problem was gone in a few days.

CHAPTER 6

Favor and Grace

We all need a favor at some point in our life. I recently told a former co-worker that he was welcome to use my name as a reference for a job he was seeking. I was contacted by the company and told them what I knew about this man. In the nine years that I had known him, it was evident that he was an excellent employee. He was punctual, had a good attitude, and did a great job. He was helpful and kind to our residents at the nursing home. I also told them that his hobby was wildlife photography. This hobby requires a lot of patience because the right moment must be captured in the snapping of the picture. He often patiently sat in the weeds, waiting for these moments. These things showed me about his character. I told them that because of these qualities, I would recommend him for any job he chose to apply for.

Not long after that, I received a call from this man. He thanked me for the recommendation and shared that it made a difference in the outcome. During his initial interview, there was no enthusiasm shown to him by the interviewer. However, after the recommendation, he received a call. He was emphatically told that they not only wanted to hire him but also wanted him to be a part of their team. Favor had been granted!

The story of Ruth and Boaz in the book of Ruth is a beautiful picture of favor. It is also a beautiful love story. Ruth was a Moabite widow who came to Israel with her mother-in-law, Naomi, who was also a widow. Every day during the harvest, Ruth went to the fields to pick up grain that had been left by the harvesters. Boaz was the landowner and happened to notice Ruth gathering grain to take home. He instructed his workers to leave plenty for her to find. She did not know Boaz but found favor in his sight. This was a tremendous blessing for her and Naomi.

The story continues, and Ruth later marries Boaz. Favor not only blessed her immediately but opened the door for greater blessings.

In the sixth chapter of Genesis, we look at the life of Noah and God's favor that was upon him. Noah was the only truly righteous man on the earth. In 2 Peter 2, he was called a preacher of righteousness. God warned Noah of the coming flood upon the world of the ungodly and made a covenant with him, promising to save him and his family. Noah was given instructions for the ark he was to build. This favor caused Noah and his family, along with pairs of animals to populate the earth, to be spared the disaster.

Because he was a preacher of righteousness, Noah probably continued to warn his neighbors that they needed to repent and give up their ungodly lifestyles. The building of this great ark was noticed by all in the area and was probably the subject of much discussion. They were not familiar with rain because the land was watered from beneath the ground. God gave these people time to repent and turn from their wicked ways, but when the ark was finished, their time was up.

The angel Gabriel told Mary that she was highly favored by God. The first chapter of Luke talks about this encounter where she was told that she would be the mother of Jesus. Mary's relative, Elizabeth, had been barren for many years. When she finally became pregnant, she acknowledged that God had given her favor. She was in her sixth month of pregnancy when Mary came to visit her.

Although Mary had favor with God, she had to deal with being pregnant before marriage to Joseph. In those days, this was highly frowned upon. Joseph was not going to marry her until an angel talked with him. And who would believe her if she said God was the father of the baby in her womb? Something like this had never happened before. Why should anyone believe her?

Look at King David before he was anointed king. David's brothers thought he was a nobody. But God turned him into somebody. Keep reading, and you will see how this incredible story unfolds.

In the book of 1 Samuel, Hannah asked God for favor because she had been unable to conceive. God honored her request, and Samuel was born. She dedicated Samuel to the Lord, and when he was weaned, she and her husband brought him to Eli, a priest, who would raise him. The Bible says that Samuel grew up in stature and in favor of the Lord and with men. Samuel became a prophet of the Lord.

The Lord sent Samuel to Bethlehem to see a man named Jesse. The Lord had chosen one of Jesse's sons to be king, and Samuel was to anoint this special one. Samuel was instructed to bring a sacrifice and invite Jesse to the sacrifice. As Jesse's sons passed in front of Samuel, none of them were chosen by the Lord. Samuel asked Jesse if these were all the sons he had. Jesse answered that his youngest son, David, was tending the sheep. Samuel asked that David be brought before him. When he arrived, the Lord told Samuel to rise and anoint him. He was the chosen one.

God's favor caused David to become king. He was a shepherd boy. His lifestyle did not look appealing to many. He spent a lot of time alone, just taking care of the sheep and protecting them from predators. However, he spent a lot of time with God, resulting in a strong relationship. This strong relationship with God helped him overcome many obstacles throughout his life. He often gave God the glory for the victories in his life. The praise and worship that he practiced as a shepherd boy continued to be an important part of his life.

Favor can cause us to stand out in the crowd. Look at the story of Esther. She was a Hebrew girl who was raised by her uncle Mordecai following the death of her parents.

King Xerxes appointed commissioners in every province of his realm to bring forth all the beautiful virgins so the king could choose his queen. Esther was one who was brought before him. There were many beautiful girls from the provinces. Esther was chosen to be the queen. She was a good queen, and King Xerxes loved her very much.

Favor helped her complete her assignment for God, and the Hebrew people, her people, were spared mass genocide.

Favor sometimes comes in unusual packages. On his way home from work one day, a friend was stopped by a police officer. He rolled down the window and handed his driver's license and proof of insurance to the officer.

The officer politely said, "Sir, you are not wearing a seat belt."

"I know, Officer," my friend softly responded. "But I have an eye issue."

"Really? You have an eye problem?"

"Yes, Officer. I cannot see myself driving with a seat belt on."

The two of them broke out in laughter. The officer returned my friend's papers, wished him a nice day, and walked back to his police car. The officer must have needed something to brighten his day.

Favor can cause us to be in the right place at the right time. It can cause us to get that job we have been wanting even though several people were applying for the same job. It can cause little blessings to come our way that we were not expecting. Let God's favor help accomplish the work in us. One of the things I like to say is, "Thank you, Lord Jesus, for the favor in my life today." I always want to be open to the goodness of God working in my life.

Grace is the unmerited, unearned love and favor of God. Whenever God acts toward us in a way we do not deserve, this is grace. God loves us so much that he continually gives us expressions of his grace. If we are born-again believers, Ephesians 2:8 tells us that God saved us by his grace when we believed and that we cannot take credit for it because it is a gift from God.

Rahab was used by God when she hid the spies at Jericho. She protected them from being captured by the enemy. By the grace of God, she and all her family were spared when the Israelites took Jericho. She was told that for her family to be protected, they had to be in her home with her. This story is in the second chapter of Joshua.

I recently taught a Bible study called "But God." These powerful two words show up throughout the Bible. We would be reading about a challenging account of someone in the Bible, and then these two words appear seemingly out of nowhere! God's intervention comes along when his people are facing insurmountable odds. He is good at that, and we see his divine intervention often. This study was not only helpful to the students, but I needed it as well. God knows how to get mileage out of his Word!

God's grace shows up and surprises us time after time. We are his children, so why wouldn't we be recipients of his unmerited favor in our lives and our circumstances? We cannot earn grace. It is a gift. When we see how giving our loving heavenly Father is, we naturally want to be givers and be a blessing to others.

Part of James 4:6 says that God opposes the proud but gives grace to the humble. In the life of Joseph, he is given many chances to become bitter and unforgiving. His story starts in Genesis 37. His brothers were very jealous of him and treated him badly. He was sold into slavery and placed in Potiphar's house. Potiphar's wife unsuccessfully tried to seduce Joseph and then lied about him, causing him to be thrown into prison. Joseph remained humble, and the grace of God worked in his life continually. He later became second in charge of Egypt and was also able to help his family during a famine. Because he chose to stay out of bitterness and unforgiveness, God was able to do great work in his life.

In the book of Exodus, Pharaoh ordered the Hebrew baby boys to be thrown into the Nile River. He feared the growing number of Hebrews would eventually greatly outnumber his Egyptian soldiers. One of these babies was Moses, who was placed in a basket among the reeds in the river. He was discovered and rescued by a daughter of Pharoah.

God's grace was with Moses. Because he was rescued by Pharoah's daughter, he was raised in the house of Pharoah. This greatly helped Moses fulfill his destiny.

Jesus was sinless, but by grace, he became our sin and went to the cross for us. Because of what Jesus did for us, by grace, God looks at us as righteous, even though we are not righteous. He looks at us through the shed blood of Jesus.

In Luke 23:34, Jesus said as he hung on the cross, "Father, forgive them." These were the people who treated him so horribly. He gave them grace.

Hebrews 4:16 is one of the scriptures I love to pray when a need arises. This is the New King James Version: "Let us therefore come boldly to the throne of grace, that we may obtain mercy and find grace to help in time of need." Many times, while praying with someone over the phone, this scripture would come forth to pray for them as well.

In a Weight Watchers meeting, there were people sharing their struggles with weight loss. This part of the meeting was more like being in a stand-up comedy show. The women took turns telling the group about the naughty things they did that week. One woman confessed that she had eaten a whole lemon meringue pie. We all agreed that sometimes we miss it, but we do not get thrown out of the program. My problem was that I like cookies. One of the members shared that this really is not a problem. Freeze the cookies and take out a few at a time. It was worth a try. However, I learned something new about myself: I like frozen cookies! I was happy to be a part of a group where grace abounds.

Grace abounds in Christianity also. We mess up at times, but God does not throw us away. He helps us get back on track and never makes us feel unworthy.

CHAPTER 7

Oh, the Upheavals in This Life!

The Bible is full of upheavals in the lives of God's people. It is also full of God helping his people overcome the upheavals. God is into the restoration business. In Jeremiah 30:17, God declares that he will restore our health and heal our wounds. Some believe that God puts sickness on people to teach them something. Our loving heavenly Father does not need to make us sick to teach us something. We have a Bible that will teach us. If we hang onto that wrong thinking, we are giving that sickness a place in our body instead of evicting it with the word of God.

We have random thoughts about the stories in the Bible. That is normal because the Bible is a big part of our lives. But sometimes, Jesus brings a story to our thoughts over and over, and we wonder why we are seeing that story repeatedly. One week, I kept thinking about the story of Jesus and the disciples on the ship. Finally, I saw what Jesus was trying to show me. God's word was coming to my rescue.

Near the end of Mark 4, Jesus was on a ship with his disciples, and he was asleep. A violent storm arose, and the disciples were afraid they were going to die, so they woke Jesus up. He spoke to the storm, and the storm obeyed him. He then said to the disciples, "Why are you so afraid? Do you still have no faith?" (Mark 4:40 NIV). They could have spoken to the storm, and it would have obeyed them.

We think how awesome that was in biblical times. The disciples had Jesus with them. He taught them, fellowshipped with them, and ate with them. Yet he asked them why they did not have faith in overcoming the storm. Here is what Jesus showed me regarding this story. Yes, they had Jesus with them in person. But we who are born again have Jesus in us. He is with us all the time. How is it that we have no faith to overcome our storms?

I recently had a major upheaval in my life. My rent increased. The price of gas went up. Groceries were more expensive. I noticed an increase in the utilities. I do not know if the rate increased or if because I was home more or if I was using them more. Whatever the reason, the increase was there. My supplemental health insurance increased. My car insurance increased. This all seemed so unfair. I saw all these increases, but my income did not increase. The storm was upon me. It took me a while to let Jesus into the boat with me. I got caught off guard and began remodeling my budget. I made some adjustments to my spending. But I was like those disciples, freaking out because the wind and the waves were crashing into me. I finally saw it. The fourth chapter of Mark came to me again, and this time, I saw that I had the answer living inside of me. Jesus lives in me. He will show me how to come out of this storm without devastation.

The first thing he showed me was that storms are temporary. They do not last forever. That was encouraging. When the Lord puts things in perspective for us, it helps us see the situation in a different way. I needed to cooperate with him, and he would lead me through the storm. He showed me little adjustments to start with. Girls' nights out would be delayed for a while. My favorite activities, movies and dining out, would be delayed as well. I went to a funeral and supported the family with my presence but had no money to put in a card. Payday was too far away. The groceries I bought were mostly necessities. Again, I was shown that this is temporary.

I asked Jesus for his help with my budget. He showed me some things I had not seen before. I had money to pay for my utilities, but the timing was not good because payday was a few days after the due date. So I post-dated the checks and wrote them out for the increased amount that was due for late payments. This was much cheaper than a bank overdraft. I called the bank regarding my credit card and reported that it would be paid on a certain date because my budget was being remodeled. The response was incredibly supportive. They saw that I was not neglecting a payment but instead delaying one for a particularly good reason. I just needed a little time to get back on track. Also, I was told that several people were experiencing the same issue because of the increases. Some adventures are more fun than others. This was not one of the fun adventures.

There are giants in the land.

Following their exodus from Egypt, the Israelites were to receive from God the Promised Land, a land flowing with milk and honey. God had promised Abraham that there would be a Promised Land for the nations to come out of his son, Isaac. Moses sent twelve scouts (one from each of the twelve tribes) into this land of Canaan to bring back a report on their findings. Ten of the twelve scouts brought back an evil report. Although the land was beautiful and would be a tremendous blessing to them, they saw giants in the land. They did not believe God would help them take the land as he promised and brought back the evil report. Joshua and Caleb, the other two scouts, brought back a good report and believed God would help them into the Promised Land. The people believed the evil report and refused to enter. Because of their disobedience, the Israelites were made to wander in the desert for forty years. They were not allowed into the Promised Land. The ten scouts who brought back the evil report were struck down with a plague and died. After forty years, Joshua and Caleb were allowed into the Promised Land. God honored their obedience. This account is found in the book of Numbers.

I was thinking about this story one morning, and the Lord said to me, "What are your giants?" This one simple question brought a flood of thoughts to my mind. What is my promised land? What blessings do I believe him for? And what hindrances am I encountering? I know God will help me receive what the Bible says is mine. I asked the Lord to show me how to cooperate with him to get to my promised land.

The attitude of the ten scouts caused their defeat. God promised his people this prosperous, beautiful land. He knew about the obstacles. He also knew they were well able to conquer the land with his help. As a child of God, I was also promised a land of milk and honey (the goodness of God in my relationship with Jesus). The devil comes to kill, steal, and destroy. Therefore, there are obstacles that try to keep me from receiving what God has for me. My refusal to claim what God has for me is, like the Israelites, a refusal to enter the Promised Land. I need to make sure my eyes are on God and not the obstacles. The giants are real. If I ignore them, I lose. God always puts things in perspective for us when we spend time with him.

One of the giants is discouragement. Why do we get discouraged? For me, discouragement comes when I look at the situation naturally and not in the spiritual. What does God's word say about my situation? I have learned over the years to talk with him about the circumstances in my life. During my conversations with him, scriptures come to my thoughts, and I write them down. We have a lot of conversations.

Sometimes, discouragement comes when we are treated unfairly. This can make us feel unappreciated or unworthy. But the truth is: I am a child of God, a blood-bought, victorious child of God. The Bible says that I can do all things through Christ who strengthens me. It also says, "Greater is he that is in me than he who is in the world." It took me a while to overcome this area, but now, I quickly forgive and turn it over to Jesus. I let go of it, and now it is his (Philippians 4:13 and 1 John 4:4).

Fear is another giant. We look at the situation and say, "What if this happens? What if I mess this up? et cetera." Take the matter to God. His thoughts are higher than ours, and his ways are higher than ours. We obviously cannot change our circumstances, but we know the ones who can. We have been told to cast our care on the Lord. He can help us in any situation. I often ask him to show me how to cooperate with him (Isaiah 55:9 and Psalms 55:22).

Another giant is walking by sight instead of faith. We often see things in the natural world, but we do not see what is going on behind the scenes in the spirit world. There were people who saw

Jesus crucified as a criminal, yet he was innocent. What they saw in the natural was horrible. What happened did not make sense to them. We need to trust God no matter what we are facing. He did not ask us to understand what was going on. He asks us to trust him. He is the great I AM. Whatever we need, he is! He is El Shaddai, the all-sufficient one. He is Jehovah Jireh, our provider. He is Jehovah Nissi, the Lord our banner. He is the Way Maker. Where there is no way, he is the way (2 Corinthians 5:7).

King David's life was full of upheavals. He wrote a lot of the psalms and talked about these upheavals and how God delivered him and protected him.

David was not born into royalty. He was a great-grandson of Ruth and Boaz. He was the youngest of Jesse's eight sons. He was a shepherd boy. He tended the sheep by himself, which shows us that he was a very responsible person. He learned a lot about survival and battle while alienated from civilization. He protected the herd from predators and was able to singlehandedly kill a lion and a bear.

David spent a lot of time playing his harp, worshipping, and visiting with God. His target practice with his slingshot helped him to become an excellent marksman.

I saw something interesting while reading the story of David's life. He was away from people, hidden away in the fields with the sheep. In nature, he looked like a nobody. Even when Samuel came to anoint one of Jesse's sons to be king, his father and brothers did not even think about him. But God loves to take the nobody and make them a somebody. God turned David into a mighty warrior. Look at Ruth. She went from a woman who gathered grain behind the reapers to the wife of a prosperous man. Look at Gideon. He saw himself as a farmer, the least in his family, to become someone great. But the angel God sent called him a mighty man of valor. God used him mightily.

David's victory over Goliath brought upheaval into his life. King Saul was jealous of him and tried to kill him many times. David had to run for his life and live in the wilderness and caves, moving around as Saul found out his locations. David had a couple of opportunities to kill Saul but chose not to because God had anointed him as king.

After Saul's death, the upheavals in David's life continued. David's sin with Bathsheba caused judgment to fall on him. Later, David was determined to take a military census of the Israelite nation. This was strictly forbidden by God. God's judgment resulted in an outbreak of disease, which killed tens of thousands of people. David repented, and the outbreak subsided.

Another upheaval occurred in David's last years as king. Adonijah, one of his sons, tried to seize the throne, but David chose Solomon as his successor.

Although David had many upheavals in his life, the Bible called him "a man after God's own heart." In 1 Samuel 13, Samuel spoke this of David. He deeply loved God, and this is expressed in the Book of Psalms. David wrote much of this book of the Bible. One of my favorites is Psalm 118:24, which says, "This is the day which the Lord has made. We will rejoice and be glad in it." It didn't matter what was coming against David; he chose to be happy, and he chose to deeply love God. This psalm always encourages me to look to God instead of my circumstances.

The devil tries to keep us from achieving what God has for us. According to Romans 8:37, we are more than conquerors through him who loved us.

God is bigger than any situation we encounter. I was awake in the middle of the night and encouraged to pray for one of my friends. All I heard was "El Shaddai." I am familiar with this, which is one of God's names. It means "more than enough." So I prayed for this friend that God would show himself as El Shaddai in his situation, whatever it was. I continued to pray for him in general and then went back to sleep. I later shared with my friend how unusual it was to receive such a short instruction for prayer. He said that was exactly what he needed and was grateful for God's intervention.

Sometimes, the upheavals in our lives are caused by poor choices. In the book of Judges, we see the life of Samson. He fell in love with a Philistine named Delilah. Samson's choice to sleep with the enemy resulted in betrayal and tragic consequences.

Delilah kept coaxing Samson to reveal to her the secret of his strength. Five Philistine leaders offered her money to find out this information. Finally, Samson told her the truth. Delilah sent for the leaders and waited for them as Samson slept on her lap. They brought a barber with them and cut his hair while he slept.

Delilah woke him up, announcing that the Philistines were going to come. Samson was not aware that the Lord had left him. The Philistines gouged out his eyes and captured him. He was taken to a prison in Gaza to grind grain.

Before long, Samson's hair began to grow again. The Philistine leaders declared a festival to celebrate the capture of Samson. He was brought from the prison and made to stand at the center of the temple between two pillars supporting the roof. The five Philistine leaders were there, as well as three thousand people on the balconies who were making fun of Samson.

Samson prayed and asked the Lord to strengthen him one more time so he could pay back the Philistines for the loss of at least one of his eyes. He also asked God to let him die with the Philistines.

God honored his prayer. Samson pushed against the two pillars, and the temple crashed down upon all the people. Those he killed at the festival were more than those he had killed during his entire life.

Jonah also experienced an upheaval in his life that was his own fault. God gave him an assignment to go to Nineveh, announcing to them that they were going to be destroyed because of their wickedness. Jonah was afraid and ran from God, getting on a ship heading in the wrong direction. The Lord caused a life-threatening storm to arise, and Jonah confessed to the crew that this was his fault because he was running from God. He instructed them to throw him overboard because they had no other choice.

A huge fish swallowed Jonah, and he stayed in the fish's belly for three days and nights. This was undoubtedly a terrifying experience. In the total darkness with seaweed wrapped around his head, Jonah did not know if he would be digested by the fish or rescued by God.

Jonah repented, pouring his heart out to the Lord, promising that he would obey him. God forgave him and caused the fish to vomit him up on dry land.

In 1 Kings 17, God told the prophet Elijah to go to Zarephath and live there. God said that he had instructed a widow to feed him.

Upon arriving at his destination, he met a widow gathering firewood and asked for a cup of water. As she went to get him a drink, he called out to her and asked for something to eat. Her response was not what he expected. She said she was almost out of food. She was going to use the firewood to cook the last meal for herself and her son, and then they would die of starvation. The upheaval in her life was off the charts!

I wondered if there were questions now in Elijah's mind. "God, did you really send me to this woman? Did I really hear from you that I was supposed to come here?"

This was his response to her: Elijah told her to first make him a biscuit and then go and cook that meal for herself and her son. God would then see to it that she never ran out of flour and oil until the drought was over. She obeyed Elijah, and the result was just as he told her. God blessed her in a way she could not imagine.

In those days, there were no food pantries to help the poor. What she told Elijah was true. They had no way to help themselves. Because God miraculously moved on her behalf, they now had a better life.

Why do bad things happen to good people? We have heard this question many times over the years. The truth is that bad things happen to all people, not just the good ones. Jesus said in John 16:33 that in this world, we will have trouble. We do not have to look far to find people who are in a lot of trouble!

CHAPTER 8

Joy

A song, "Mr. Bojangles," was on my mind one morning as I woke up. I had not heard that song in a long time. It kept playing in my mind as I got dressed for work and made my breakfast. "Okay, Jesus, what is up with this song?" I read the lyrics and then continued getting ready for work.

Sitting at my desk, the Lord spoke to me. "That song is a picture of joy. Many people don't really know what joy is." I know that some things cannot be learned by studying the subject. They must be experienced. Joy is not really the same thing as happiness. Happiness is temporary, but joy is so deep that it is there even when we are going through hard times. Joy is more like contentment, a deep satisfaction, like happiness on steroids!

The writer of this song was a country singer, Jerry Jeff Walker. He met Mr. Bojangles (Bill Robinson) in a jail cell in New Orleans. His neighboring cellmates often asked him to dance for them to lighten the atmosphere of their surroundings. He was happy to dance for them. He told Jerry that he often spent time in jail because of his drinking. Jerry was fascinated with this man and wrote a song about him when he returned home.

Bill had an interesting life. His parents died when he was a child, and he was raised by his grandmother. At eight years old, he started dancing for pennies. He was a gifted dancer and later appeared in many movies. Although he had great success, he had a lot of heartache throughout his life. As an old man, he was homeless, but he never stopped dancing. That gift brought joy to his life no matter what he was going through. No one could steal that joy from him. His ragged clothing and life on the street did not define him. His dancing kept the joy springing up within him. Nothing was said in the articles about whether he was a Christian, but he used the gift God gave him, and the joy that gift brought him was evident throughout his life.

Several years ago, I had a prayer partner named Betty. She and her husband owned a small motel, and their house was connected to one end of it. Betty was not only interested in her customers' business, but she cared about them personally. If something was not going well in their lives, she was quick to offer to pray with them and get God involved in their situation. She went the extra mile for them. She often hung the bed sheets outside so they would have that fresh air smell. When she made cookies, she made enough to share with her overnight guests. She would leave a plate of cookies in their rooms so they would encounter a blessing when they walked through the door.

At times, while having lunch together, we would be visiting about things going on in our lives or in town, and she would say, "Well, let's pray about that right now!" She would not even wait till lunch was over! I loved that about her. It was obvious that joy was a big part of her life. It did not matter what was going on in her life. Joy was there.

My most intense encounter with joy was in childbirth. There were complications both times, and the pain was almost unbearable. But the joy that was present when my children were born was far greater than any pain I experienced. Only God could provide that.

Sometimes, people think that when they go through hard times, they have done something wrong, and God is punishing them. Second Timothy 2:3 reminds us that we must endure hardship as a good soldier of Jesus Christ. We live in a world where a lot of bad things happen. God is not punishing us. One of the last things Jesus told his disciples was that they would suffer persecution and hardships. Look at what he said to them: "I have told you all this so that you may have peace in me. Here on earth, you will have many trials and sorrows. But take heart because I have overcome the world" (John 16:33 NLT). In the Amplified version, it says to be filled with joy. So we must use our faith to get to the other side of this. Victory does not just land on us. How do we have joy when it looks like our world is falling apart? By focusing on the answer instead of the problem. We have let our feelings take too much charge of our lives.

God could have kept Daniel out of the lion's den. He could have kept Paul and Silas out of jail. He could have kept Shadrach, Meshach, and Abednego out of King Nebuchadnezzar's fiery furnace. These men were greatly loved by God, but he allowed them to go through these trials in their lives.

We can have victory in trials. We are told in James 1:2–4 (NKJV) to count it all joy when we fall into various trials, knowing that the testing of our faith produces patience. But let patience have its perfect work, that we may be perfect and complete, lacking nothing. How can we have joy when we are experiencing trials? We need to stay close to the Lord so we encounter victory instead of a disaster. Proof of this is in Ephesians 6:10–12 (NLT): "A final word: Be strong in the Lord and in his mighty power. Put on all of God's armor so that you will be able to stand firm against all strategies of the devil. For we are not fighting against flesh-and-blood enemies but against evil rulers and authorities of the unseen world, against mighty powers in this dark world, and against evil spirits in the heavenly places." After these verses, a description of the armor of God is shown to us. We know God is working in our lives, and we have a destiny to fulfill. If we are in a trial, God has a purpose for it.

David's life is an example of joy. Even amid all the upheavals in his life, he never stopped praising and worshipping God. When we need encouragement, the Psalms are a good place to start. We see how David pours his heart out to the Lord, and we are encouraged to do the same. "You will show me the way of life, granting me the joy of your presence and the pleasures of living with you forever" (Psalms 16:11 NLT).

Have you ever noticed that when your day is filled with chaos and anxiety, a heart-to-heart talk with the Lord makes it all better?

What is interesting is that we try to figure it out ourselves, getting nowhere, and then when we take it before the Lord, he helps us. I laughed when I saw this scripture because it was talking about me. "When anxiety was great within me, your consolation brought me joy" (Psalms 94:19 NIV).

In the twelfth chapter of Hebrews, it says that for the joy that was set before Jesus, he endured the cross, despising the shame. We know that Jesus was tortured for us so that we could be free. Yet, the word "joy" was used, even though everything he went through was horrible. There was no mercy given to him. What this shows us is that joy is so powerful; we can have joy in the worst of circumstances.

Jesus knew what awaited him. He spent some time in prayer in the Garden of Gethsemane. He was in anguish, and his sweat was like drops of blood. He said this, "Father, if you are willing, please take this cup of suffering away from me. Yet I want your will to be done, not mine" (Luke 22:42 NLT). He had a choice and decided we were worth it. I will be forever grateful for his sacrifice. Jesus is our example of joy. 1 Peter 1:8 (NLT) says, "You love him even though you have never seen him. Though you do not see him now, you trust him, and you rejoice with a glorious, inexpressible joy."

We all know how hard it is to be joyful when we are going through unpleasant circumstances. Yet we are told in James 1:2 (NLT) to consider it an opportunity for great joy when troubles of any kind come our way. So in trying to be positive, the first thought that comes to me is to be thankful that this trouble is temporary. We never have a victory without a battle. I needed to reevaluate the way I was looking at trials. I now see them as an opportunity to grow and learn something in the experience. Negativity does not produce positive things, so I knew I needed to keep a positive attitude. How can we pass the test if the test never comes? How can we develop spiritual stamina if hardship never arrives? How can we overcome if there is nothing to overcome? Testing is necessary.

One of my encounters with joy was at the passing of my mother. We were not only mother and daughter, but we were best friends. Although my heart was flooded with grief and sadness, I noticed that joy was also present, reminding me of the good times we had together. That joy strengthened me so that I could make it through the funeral service without falling apart.

I recently led a Bible study for the Assisted Living section of the nursing home. I do not use the packaged, ready-to-teach outlines. I ask the Lord what he wants me to share since he knows the residents better than I do. He gave me the topic, "Grow where you are planted." Although this subject was perfect for them, I found that as I put the presentation together, it was valuable for anyone. Basically, this is what I shared with them:

God knows where you are. Many times, we feel like we are stuck here, and that is just the way life is. But God created us for a purpose. We have a destiny (Jeremiah 29:11), and he didn't leave anyone out. Here's my point: We are here right now for the time being. It could change at any time, but while we are here, we can grow where we are planted!

Sometimes, it is the little things that make a difference in a person's day. Lunch was dropped off at my front desk one day. A sandwich and onion rings were still hot, and I was excited.

I glanced down the hall and saw one of my coworkers. A strong thought flashed through my mind: Give her some of those onion rings! As she came into my area, I held up the bag and exclaimed, "You need to help me with these onion rings!" She turned and walked up to my desk. "Are you serious? I love onion rings!" I encouraged her to take several because I was given too many.

This small act of kindness made her smile. I later learned that she was having a hard day. I was so thankful to be tuned into the Holy Spirit that day. It made my day as well as hers. How did I know that was the Holy Spirit? Because I do not offer to share my lunch.

We need to take advantage of the opportunities in life and be grateful in our present situation, for the Bible says, "In everything give thanks" (1 Thess. 5:18). It does not say to give thanks for everything but to give thanks in everything. So if we are in difficult circumstances, we can still give thanks to the Lord while we are going through it. For example, we are not thankful for a disease, but we are thankful that the Lord is helping us to get well.

There are things you can do to thrive even amidst circumstances that are not ideal. First, we need a good attitude. Try to see something positive in the situation and make the most of it every day. In John 10:10, we are shown that the thief's purpose is to steal and kill and destroy, but God's purpose is to give us a rich and satisfying life. God really does want the best for us.

Joy filled my heart as my daughter's wedding date was approaching. Angie picked me up one Saturday, and we headed for Omaha to find shoes for the wedding. Shoes are expensive, so I prayed for the Lord's help in finding the right shoes, and I did not want to pay over $30. The first place we stopped had a shoe sale! Angie saw the perfect pair and brought them over to show me. They were beautiful but half a size too small. As I looked at them, I remarked that they looked like the right size. I tried them on, and they fit perfectly. The original price was $60, and they were on sale for $29. I said to the cashier, "I am so excited! I found these shoes, and they are on sale!" He said, "And I am excited for you!"

I got back to the car, smiling and saying to the Lord, "Thank you. You did this for me." I immediately heard this scripture in my spirit: "Now unto him that is able to do exceedingly abundantly above all that we ask or think, according to the power that works in us" (Eph. 3:20 KJV). I had not thought of that scripture in a long time, but it was perfect for the occasion!

The joy continued. After the wedding, I had some days off work and was able to babysit their dog while they were away. It was a fun time for all of us, even the dog!

What I have noticed about joy is that there is contentment with it.

In the first chapter of Luke, there is an unusual picture of joy in the story where an angel tells Mary she is going to give birth to Jesus and then tells her that her relative, Elizabeth, is pregnant and in her sixth month. Mary went to visit Elizabeth, who was pregnant with John the Baptist. When Mary greeted her, the scripture says the baby in her womb leaped for joy. Who would think that a baby in the womb could express joy? But that is what the Bible says.

Christmas season had arrived, and the nursing home was decorated with beautiful trees, decorations, and lights. The local Lutheran church invited our residents to a joy-filled celebration of the birth of Jesus. That was so nice of them to think of us and include us in their festivities. One of our residents walked by my desk and announced that she would not be attending because it was not a Catholic function. She was not expecting my response to be in the form of a sermon, but that is what she got. There are no denominations in heaven, so maybe we can celebrate together while we are on this earth. We love the same Jesus. Some of the residents complain that they do not have anywhere to go, but when they get a chance to go somewhere, they turn down the invitation. It was nice that some would go and enjoy the celebration.

A resident stopped by my desk one afternoon and thanked me for leading church every week. I teach a Bible study three times a week, and she calls it church. She smiled and said she talks to the Lord throughout the day now because I told the class that I talk to him a lot during the day. He is with us all the time, so we should acknowledge him. It made my heart happy to know that someone was blessed by the Bible study.

Some people think that happiness and joy are the same thing. Happiness occurs when something pleasant is experienced in our familiar surroundings. Joy makes our hearts happy. It comes from deep within. It is there even when we experience times of hardship. Happiness leaves during those times.

"This is the day that the Lord has made. I will rejoice and be glad in it" (Psalms 118:24). This scripture reminds me that, no matter what is going on around me, I can choose to be joyful every day.

We can increase our joy and the joy of others by simply choosing to say good things. Positive, thankful thoughts do not happen by accident. We must, on purpose, practice them. "A happy heart is good medicine, and a joyful mind causes healing, but a broken spirit dries up the bones" (Proverbs 17:22 AMPC). There is a section called "Laughter, the Best Medicine" in the Reader's Digest. They now have compiled these into books!

Difficulty is never welcomed, but right thinking will cheer us up. The older I get, the more I am convinced that joy comes more from what I believe than from what is happening around me. How can we have joy when it looks like our world is falling apart? By focusing on the answer instead of the problem. We often let our feelings have too much control over our lives.

One day, I was reading a book by Smith Wigglesworth. He shared about a few people from church who went to a man's house to pray for him. He had been in bed for several days and welcomed the visit from his friends. They prayed and prayed, expecting him to be healed. After a while, they left and stood outside his house, talking about the disappointing results. One of the men said that their focus had been on the man and his condition. He commented that their focus should have been on the name of Jesus and not the condition because the name of Jesus is above every name, including the sickness that had attacked their friend. The group went back to their friend's bedroom and focused on the name of Jesus instead of his condition. Their prayer strategy changed the outcome, and in a very short time, he was healed. This exciting encounter not only brought joy to the man but also to the prayer team!

Can you imagine the joy Sarah experienced when Isaac was born? She was ninety years old when she gave birth to Isaac! Look what she said when she was told she would be the mother of many nations: "Sarah said, God has brought me laughter, and everyone who hears about this will laugh with me" (Genesis 21:6 NIV). This child was named well. His name means laughter.

The parable of the prodigal son in Luke 15 is a beautiful picture of joy. The son did not want to wait until his father died to receive his inheritance. He wanted to enjoy it now. So, the father gave his two sons their inheritance early. This son went away and lived a reckless life. After a while, his money ran out, and no one would help him. Feeling sorrowful for the choices he had made, he returned home penniless. His father saw him coming at a distance, and great joy filled his heart. He prepared a banquet and celebration after seeing that his son was coming home!

Although trials can be unpleasant, there is joy in knowing that I am God's child and he is working in my life. Because joy is one of the fruits of the Holy Spirit, it is important for it to be a part of my life.

I was recently invited to an event with Great Plains Pilgrimage, which was taking place not far from my home. I had never been to a church retreat, so I was excited to experience this.

There were a lot of people at the campground. Seven of us were called "guests" because it was our first time on a pilgrimage. We were never alone there. One of the people who knew what was going on was always by our side, helping us to participate and be an active part of the group. We attended chapel services and listened to several speakers from different churches. Others made sure we had water or coffee or whatever we would like to make our experience more enjoyable. Love was continually poured out upon us.

It did not stop there. At bedtime, we were met with a gift bag on the bed and a few small gifts with scripture and encouraging words on the pillow. There was an essential oil spray to spray the pillow to ensure a good night's sleep! The smell was wonderful, and I did sleep well.

We sat at tables so we could talk about the subject we heard. The exchange of ideas was refreshing, and it helped us get to know each other better as the weekend went on. The dining hall was not far from our building. The scenery was beautiful, and the food was delicious.

We also did some skits about the subjects that were shared. These were funny, and we saw that laughter was part of the weekend.

Although grace was the main theme of this event, my description would be a different word: Joy, pure joy. What an amazing experience!

CHAPTER 9

Wisdom

Wisdom must be something incredibly special because King Solomon asked God for it, and it pleased the Lord. The Lord not only granted his request but added to it. King Solomon's motive was pure. He wanted wisdom to help him in governing the kingdom. King Solomon wrote most of the book of Proverbs. Motives are particularly important to God. We should always check our motives before praying for something. Asking for wisdom may cause revelation to come regarding why I am going through difficult circumstances. I also ask God to help me learn from my experiences so I do not make the same mistakes over and over. In Ecclesiastes, it says that God gives wisdom, knowledge, and joy to those who please him (Ecclesiastes 2:26 NLT).

"A scoffer seeks wisdom and finds none [for his ears are closed to wisdom], but knowledge is easy for one who understands [because he is willing to learn]" (Proverbs 14:6 AMP). A scoffer is a person who is verbally disrespectful, and because of that character flaw, he is not willing to change to get wisdom. Sometimes, scoffers are disrespectful because they do not understand the truth. The Lord loves a humble person who is thankful for the word of God.

If you need wisdom, ask our generous God,
and he will give it to you. He will not rebuke you
for asking. But when you ask him, be sure that

your faith is in God alone. Do not waver, for a person with divided loyalty is as unsettled as a wave of the sea that is blown and tossed by the wind. Such people should not expect to receive anything from the Lord. Their loyalty is divided between God and the world, and they are unstable in everything they do. (James 1:5–8 NLT)

One of the stories that is dear to my heart is found in 2 Chronicles 20. Jehoshaphat, King of Judah, is facing a raging battle, and he needs God's wisdom. He knows the odds are against him, and his army is greatly outnumbered. He needed strategy and direction. The Lord said the battle is not Jehoshaphat's but his. His army would show up but would not be fighting. When they showed up, what they saw were dead bodies. The armies that were coming against them fought each other. The Lord sent ambushments against the enemy, and the Lord won that battle. It took Jehoshaphat's men three days to get what they wanted to take home from the victory. The Lord not only gave Jehoshaphat wisdom, but he also fought the battle for him. God always wins.

All the battles we face are not short-lived ones. Some are long, raging battles, and we need the wisdom of God to help us to be victorious. The wisdom of God helps us to make the right decisions along the way and to see things from the right perspective. God's thoughts are higher than ours, and his ways are higher than ours, according to Isaiah 55:9. Jehoshaphat had no idea how the Lord was going to fight for him, but he chose to trust him.

In the book of Judges, we see Samson's story. He should have asked God for wisdom but instead made some very bad choices, and it brought devastating circumstances to his life. I shared his story in chapter 7.

I learned about wisdom the hard way. God was trying to show me some things to help me, and I did not realize it was him. I was a new Christian but wanted to learn how to have more of God in my life. Some friends and I went to a restaurant one night and visited the salad bar before our meal arrived. I touched the spoon of one of the salads, and a very strong thought flashed through my mind: "Don't eat that one." I overrode that thought with one of my own: "I love this salad. This is one of my favorites!" In the middle of the night, I was awakened by projectile vomiting. An image of that salad and the warning flashed through my mind. I now realized that was not just a fleeting thought. It was the Holy Spirit trying to protect me! Wisdom helps us make better choices. I decided to pay more attention to my thoughts now.

Nine years into my marriage, I attended a church service that presented a salvation message, and I came forward for prayer, asking Jesus into my life. In that salvation experience, I was given a passion to pray for people. After forty years, that passion is still strong. I bought several books about prayer so I could learn how to pray for myself and other people. I studied and practiced what I learned. I prayed a lot for my marriage, confident that our marriage would be healed. God was merciful and helped me as much as he could, but I would not let go of the marriage.

After thirty-six years of marriage, I finally learned that God was not in our marriage. He did not bring us together. We chose each other. We did not know God and, therefore, did not seek him regarding our choices. Although part of the wedding vows says, "What God has joined together," God is not necessarily a part of the relationship. I needed to move on with my life, and I filed for divorce.

Although I learned a lot about prayer, wisdom was not part of the curriculum. Although the marriage was not a good one, the healing process afterward was magnificent. I had no money to pay a therapist, so Jesus was my therapist. I knew I needed a lot of emotional healing, and the unraveling began. In my books, *Get Real with God* and *Progressive Healing*, I have shared many stories that others can relate to. Along with the stories is the remedy used for getting the desired results. I wanted to be free, and I often spoke that to Jesus as I poured my heart out before him. I remembered that in the fourth chapter of James, it says, "You have not because you ask not," so I was continually asking for help.

I learned about wisdom as I continued to study, and this made a difference in the healing process. I started asking for wisdom in a lot of areas. I found a new tool.

Being honest with ourselves is also wise. Suppose we think we have forgiven someone, and we continue to speak negatively about them. Part of Matthew 12:34 says that the mouth speaks what the heart is full of. When we catch ourselves speaking unkindly about others, we need to look inside and see what is in our hearts. Are we bitter, offended, hurt, angry, or jealous? The Holy Spirit will help us if we let him. Do not wait until next week to deal with this. Repent and ask the Lord to forgive you and tell him you forgive that one who hurt you. Not dealing with these issues can cause a lack of sleep, tiredness, and sickness. We need to get healed on the inside so we can enjoy our lives.

"Walk with the wise and become wise; associate with fools and get in trouble" (Prov. 13:20 NLT). When I was in high school, my mother used to tell me that birds of a feather flock together and to be careful who I became friends with. If I chose friends who had bad reputations, I would also have a bad reputation even if I was innocent. My mother was a wise woman.

The first part of Proverbs 9:10 says that the fear of the Lord is the beginning of wisdom. When I first read this, I was unsure what to think. I wanted wisdom but did not know what to think about being afraid of God, knowing that he is our loving heavenly Father. The *Merriam-Webster Dictionary* could shed some light on this. I was pleasantly surprised when I saw one of the definitions of fear: profound reverence and awe, especially toward God. So now, I do not have to be afraid of God.

Hebrews 12:5–11 describes God's discipline of the believer. While it is done in love, it is still a fearful thing. The New Living Translation says it this way: "Have you forgotten the encouraging words God spoke to you as his children? He said, 'My child, don't make light of the Lord's discipline, and don't give up when he corrects you.'"

This reminds me of being corrected by my parents when I was a child. There were five children in our family, and there were chaotic times when Mom yelled upstairs and said, "Don't make me come up there!" She only had to say it once! We knew she loved us, and we knew we needed correction at times.

Now I am older and wiser, but I still get naughty at times. I remember Valentine's Day, sitting in my favorite chair with an assortment of unbelievably delicious chocolate. Sometimes, we wish God would turn his head for a little while. But this thought came trotting through my mind: "You know you need to repent for gluttony." He was right, and I have made some progress over the years. I need to work on moderation.

The right fear of God is a blessing of the new covenant. The Lord promised in Jeremiah 32 that he would give his people one heart and one way so that they would fear him forever, for their own good and the good of their children after them.

In the eleventh chapter of Isaiah, talking about Jesus, it says that his delight is in the fear of the Lord. So, we see that even Jesus had the fear of God. We would be wise to do the same.

God offers to help us with wisdom. In Psalm 32:8, he said he would instruct, counsel, and teach us in the way we should go. He has a wonderful destiny for all of us, and it would be wise of us to include him in our lives. Wisdom is not about knowing all the answers. It is about knowing the One who knows the answers.

CHAPTER 10

It Is Written

These three words are so powerful. Jesus did not need many words to get his point across to the devil. In the fourth chapter of Matthew, Jesus is tested by the devil in the wilderness. Three times, the devil tempted him, and three times, Jesus answered by saying, "It is written," and followed with scripture. As children of almighty God, we can use scripture regarding our circumstances. Even if you do not know much scripture, there are a few basic ones you can start with till you get used to praying. I still use these at times. Here are a few of my favorites: "Greater is he that is in you, than he that is in the world." This is the last part of 1 John 4:4. In Philippians 2, we are reminded that Jesus has the name that is above every name. "Submit yourselves, then, to God. Resist the devil, and he will flee from you" (James 4:7 NIV). So basically, here is how I pray, using the teaching from Jesus:

> Father, in the name of Jesus, I come to you. Because I am your child, I have the greater one living inside of me. And Jesus has given me his name to use against the enemy. So, devil, I say to you, it is written, greater is he that is in me than he that is in the world. It is also written that the name of Jesus is above every name. His name is above your name, devil. And the one that lives in

me is greater than you. I am submitted to God, and I resist you in the name of Jesus and with the blood of Jesus. So, you get your hands off my health. Get your hands off my finances. Get your hands off my family. Loose your hold of God's property, which I am. Jesus shed his blood for me, and I am a blood-bought child of God. Go now, in the name of Jesus.

Honor your father and your mother so that you may live long in the land the Lord your God is giving you. This scripture is found in Exodus 20:12. Some of us find this verse disturbing because of an abusive childhood. How does a person honor someone who has treated them so cruelly over the years?

According to Romans 8:28, we can trust God, our heavenly father, to heal those wounds and live a fulfilling life, not crippled by the past. If we come to him and simply ask him for help in forgiving those who have hurt us, he will. He is no respecter of persons, and he will not make you wait until you think you are cleaned up enough to approach him. Do not wait. Do it now. Come to him simply because God is not a difficult God, and pray something like this:

Father, in the name of Jesus, I come to you and ask for your help in forgiving my parents who have hurt me as a child. I choose to forgive them for all they have done to me. Thank you, Father. Amen.

That opened the door for healing of the wounds you have suffered over the years. Forgiveness does not mean that you agree with their mistreatment. It means you forgive what they did to you, and you turn it over to God. It belongs to him now. Let go of it.

Forgiveness does not mean that now you are best buddies. God does not expect you to go back into that toxic relationship. We are not expected to put ourselves in harm's way.

Do not be afraid to be honest with God. He wants to help you. He does not want us carrying that baggage from the past. You may think that because it was so many years ago, it does not matter anymore. The wounds are there, and it does matter. There is no expiration date on healing our wounds.

We should never feel guilty for staying away from abusive parents. You can honor them from a distance by forgiving them in prayer and then praying for their salvation. Remember, God has it now, so you can let it go.

There are weeks when I feel like I am wearing out a scripture because of using it often. Sometimes in night, I would wake up with pain from stretching wrong while changing positions in bed. I would be wide awake, and a scripture was handy. It is written in Psalm 50:15: "Call on you, Lord, when I'm in trouble, and you will rescue me, and I will honor you. So I am calling on you because I am in trouble with this pain, and I need to go to work in a few hours. Please, Lord, take the pain away. In Jesus's name, I thank you and give you the praise and the glory for my victory. Amen."

Hebrews 4:16 is another scripture that I keep ready. I start praying and speaking the scripture, followed by what I need for that time. I have received God's help with this one scripture many times: "Let us, therefore, come boldly unto the throne of grace, that we may obtain mercy, and find grace to help in time of need." I tell God what I need, thank him, and go to sleep. "This is the confidence that we have in Him, that if we ask anything according to his will, he hears us. And if we know that he hears us, whatever we ask, we know that we have the petitions that we have asked of him" (1 John 5:14–15 NKJV). In my desperation, I cried out to him many times, knowing that in a few hours, I needed to get up and go to work. He never let me down.

I was studying the root of bitterness. This study was of interest to me because, over the years, I had forgiven so much that I was sure my forgiver was worn out! Hebrews 12:15 reminds us to see to it that we do not fall short of the grace of God because a root of bitterness can spring up, causing trouble for us. The Amplified version calls it a root of resentment.

It is written that the heart is deceitful and desperately wicked (Jer. 17:9). Although I was unaware of any bitterness in my life, I knew that a deceitful heart would not tell on itself. Therefore, I asked the Holy Spirit to show me any bitterness in my heart. He does not always give me immediate answers, so I put my request before him and went on with my daily activities.

Over the next few days, a flash from the past would come to mind. It was like a short movie clip. At the end, I heard the word "bitterness." After praying through what I was shown, I took it a step further and asked Jesus to pull out of my cellular memory the negative emotions related to the experiences I saw. There is a chapter about cellular memory in my previous book, *Progressive Healing*, so I will not go into detail here.

There are many who have not dealt with hurt from the past. Self-deception has told them that it is done and over, and they move on with their lives, pushing aside the resentment and pain left behind. I was one of those people. As the Holy Spirit showed me, I prayed and forgave anew, knowing that it was my desire to walk in love. I am grateful that we cannot overdose on prayer!

Isaiah 54:17 is a scripture I often use in prayer. It says that no weapon formed against me shall prosper. The enemy has many weapons that he uses against us: sickness, lack, discouragement, fear, deception, disappointment, lies, etc. Our weapons are far greater than his. We have the name of Jesus and the blood of Jesus.

I was awakened in the night by sinus congestion. A few seconds later, I saw a vision of the stripes on the back of Jesus. They were not just stripes as I had seen pictured in different articles. They were deep and bleeding profusely. Jesus was paying the price for my healing. I had never seen a picture like this.

I addressed the issue with a quick prayer: "Father, in the name of Jesus, I apply the blood of Jesus to my sinuses, for it is written that by his stripes I was healed." I fell asleep and enjoyed the rest of the night uninterrupted.

Nahum 1:9—the last part of this scripture is one you will want to wear out! The Holy Spirit has brought this word to me many times because some of the afflictions I have been healed of have tried to come back, and this scripture deals with that issue. The New King James Version says, "…affliction will not rise up a second time."

For a few weeks, there was mild pain in my upper arm. It was more of an ache than a pain. I did some stretches and prayed for healing. Then one night, as I turned on my side in bed, it was more noticeable. These words came to me: "Frozen shoulder is trying to revisit you." A couple of years ago, I was diagnosed with a frozen shoulder, and twelve weeks of physical therapy and prayer kept me from having surgery.

This news from the Holy Spirit made me so angry at the devil for trying to bring this back on my body. So in the middle of the night, this is basically how my rant against the devil went: "Devil, I stand against you in the name of Jesus, the name that is above every name, and that name is above your name. I have been healed of a frozen shoulder, and you are not stealing it from me. It is written in Nahum 1:9 that affliction shall not rise a second time. So you have no right to afflict me. You have trespassed on God's property, which I am. My body is the temple of the Holy Spirit, and you must leave. So go in the name of Jesus!" It took a few days to leave, but I did not give up. I kept commanding him to leave.

Several years ago, I was healed of plantar fasciitis. The symptom recently returned, and I took care of it with Nahum 1:9. This was easier to spot than the ache in my arm because the sudden pain in my heel quickly reminded me of the affliction I was healed of. I confronted the devil, and the symptoms left.

Some people who are not familiar with this scripture unknowingly let a previously healed affliction come back on them. They think, "Well, I thought I was healed, but I must not have been." They think God let them down, but they opened the door for it to return by not standing their ground against the devil.

God did not promise that we would understand things. He asked us to trust him (Prov. 3:5–6). We are told in Romans 8:28 that all things work together for good for those who are called according to his purpose. We will have times of difficulty, but remember that this is temporary. The devil did not leave Jesus alone, and he does not leave us alone.

God's word is not skin deep. It goes right to the innermost parts of our being. It can cut through all the junk in our lives. It can judge our motives, which are especially important to God, and our attitude, which often needs to be adjusted. This is clearly shown in Hebrews 4:12 (NIV): "For the word of God is living and active. Sharper than any double-edged sword, it penetrates even to dividing soul and spirit, joints, and marrow; it judges the thoughts and attitudes of the heart."

Our lives have become compromised because the lies of the devil have become louder than the Word of God. The deceiver has taken more of our time than Jesus. Our thoughts have been more on the affliction than the healer. We can make an adjustment in our thinking. God is not difficult. He wants us to prosper.

When I was a new Christian, I worked in a doctor's office. Doctors ask the patients about diseases that tend to run down their family line. This was my introduction to the subject of generational curses. As I worked on the patient files, I saw several diseases that were generational. This was an excellent job for me because I practiced praying for the patients as I worked on their files. I also learned a lot about medical conditions.

We receive generational blessings as well as curses. We get an inheritance of physical traits, talents, and interests from our family line.

The Bible has some things to say about generational curses. I learned that the devil has the right to block healing if there is a generational curse involved. The curse needs to be broken so that healing can come. However, not all diseases are accompanied by a generational curse.

In the four years volunteering at the Healing Rooms, we prayed for several people regarding generational curses. They are not difficult to break. Proverbs 26:2 says the curse causeless shall not come. Exodus 20:5 tells us that God will bring punishment to the third and fourth generations. These scriptures clearly showed us the activity of the generational curse. We asked Jesus to forgive the ancestors of the patient for the sin they committed that opened the door for this curse to come into the family and travel down the bloodline of the family. We thanked Jesus for forgiveness and asked him to put his blood on that sin. We then closed the door of entry and sealed it with the blood of Jesus. We then addressed the devil: "Devil, the curse has been broken, and the door of entry is now sealed with the blood of Jesus. You no longer have a right to afflict this person with cancer (or whatever disease). You no longer have the right to afflict your children and future generations. Now go in the name of Jesus." We then prayed for healing.

The generational curse gave the devil the right to keep the disease on the person, and we needed to cancel that right.

"It is finished." These were the last words that Jesus spoke before he died on the cross for us. This is found in John 19:30. Jesus completed all he was sent to do. He took our place on the cross and reconciled us back to Father God. Now when God looks at us, he looks at us through the shed blood of Jesus.

CHAPTER 11

Forgiveness

We have all heard people say, "I'll never forgive ___ for what they did." What they did not realize was that they were not hurting the offender. They were hurting themselves.

The Bible has some uncomfortable things to say about unforgiveness. It says that if we do not forgive, God will not forgive us.

It was hard to overcome unforgiveness in my life. There is a lot of pain, different kinds of pain, attached to unforgiveness. But as the Lord brought me through a lot of emotional healing, I was able to forgive. He gave me beauty for ashes. I spent a lot of one-on-one time with Jesus, and that time is priceless.

During the hardest times of forgiveness, I remembered Jesus hanging on the cross saying, "Father, forgive them, for they don't know what they are doing" (Luke 23:34). My suffering was not anything like what he suffered, and yet he forgave. Therefore, I could forgive. When we truly forgive, we let go of it and turn it over to Jesus. We mistakenly think that the offender is off the hook. No, Jesus takes care of it his way, which is better than our way. For his ways are higher than ours, and his thoughts are higher than ours (Isaiah 55:8–9).

Unforgiveness can be a roadblock to healing because it is a sin. Sin separates us from God, so if we are participating in sin, how can we expect God to help us? So remember, that unforgiveness you are holding in your heart is not hurting anyone but you.

Some say they hold grudges but do not have unforgiveness. It is the same thing but with a different label.

The devil wants to keep us in unforgiveness because it robs us of our blessings. Sin separates us from God, and if we let unforgiveness reign in our lives, he cannot bless us to the extent he wants to.

If you are having trouble in this area, look at the story of Joseph starting in Genesis 37. Joseph's brothers, who hated him and were very jealous of him, were away from home to graze their father's flocks. His father sent him to check on his brothers and to bring word back to him of how they were doing. When they saw him at a distance, they plotted to kill him and throw him into a cistern. Then they were going to tell their father that a ferocious animal devoured him. Reuben, one of the brothers, talked them out of killing Joseph. They took off his robe and threw him into the cistern, which had no water in it and left him there to die. Reuben left and planned to come back and rescue him later. As the other brothers sat down to eat, they saw a caravan of Ishmaelites, who were also called Midianites, on their way to Egypt. The brothers decided to sell Joseph instead of leaving him there to die. They killed a goat and dipped Joseph's robe in the blood as proof to their father that he had been killed.

Joseph already had plenty of reasons to be in unforgiveness toward his brothers. His story continues.

Joseph was taken to Egypt and sold to an Egyptian, who was one of Pharoah's officials, named Potiphar. The Lord's favor continued to be with Joseph, and he did well in Potiphar's house. When Potiphar saw that the Lord was with Joseph and everything he did was successful, he put Joseph in charge of his household, and everything he owned was put in Joseph's care. Favor was abounding in Joseph's life.

Potiphar's wife tried to entice Joseph to come to bed with her, but he kept refusing. She lied to her husband about Joseph mistreating her, and Joseph ended up in prison, where the king's prisoners were in confinement. Joseph could have easily been unforgiving toward her but chose against it. Favor continued, even though Joseph was in prison. God granted him favor with the prison warden, who put him in charge of all who were in the prison.

The king's cupbearer and the baker were among those held in prison. They both had a dream one night and were sad the next day because they did not know what the dreams meant. Joseph told them that interpretations belong to God, and he interpreted the dreams for them. The cupbearer's dream meant that Pharoah would restore him to his position in three days. Joseph asked that he remember this kindness and mention him to Pharoah so he could be released from prison. The cupbearer forgot about Joseph. He passed up another opportunity to be in unforgiveness.

Two years passed, and Pharoah had a dream and wondered what it meant. The cupbearer told him about Joseph interpreting his and the baker's dreams. Things turned out exactly as the interpretation said. Joseph was quickly brought before Pharoah. God showed Joseph what the dream meant, and he explained it to Pharoah, along with instructions to protect Egypt from famine. Pharoah extended favor to Joseph and put him in charge of his palace. All the people were to submit to his orders. Joseph was now in charge of Egypt! Favor not only caused him to thrive but Egypt was blessed as well. If Joseph had allowed himself to have unforgiveness in his life, these blessings would not have come upon him.

Because Joseph continued to keep unforgiveness and bitterness out of his life, favor continually followed him. We see in this incredible story that the Lord does not always take us out of the problem but, instead, takes us through the problem.

I recently noticed some thoughts that kept creeping into my mind. They were negative thoughts about a person. I kept pushing them away, knowing that I had already forgiven them. Later in my prayer time, I asked the Lord why I kept hearing those thoughts. I knew I had forgiven, but maybe I missed something. The Lord said, "Yes, you have forgiven. But there are soul wounds that need to be healed. In the natural, it looks like this: you forgave, but you are still bleeding." Now it made sense to me. It really is very simple to take care of this. In this situation, my prayer was simple and effective:

Father, in the name of Jesus, I come to you.
I have forgiven this person, and now I am ask-

ing you to heal the wounds in my soul from the incident involved. The scripture tells us that we were healed by your stripes, Jesus. That healing includes soul healing. So, thank you, Lord, for healing these soul wounds. I am always grateful for your help in my life. Amen.

There is a chapter about healing the soul in my last book, *Progressive Healing*. It is comforting to know that healing goes beyond the physical.

CHAPTER 12

Love

The Bible tells us that God is love. God gets blamed for a lot of things that are not his fault. Wickedness is not his nature. One of the residents made a comment in Bible study about the verse that says the Lord gives and the Lord takes away. My response was that this statement was not made by the Lord. Job made that statement, not knowing that God did not cause all that trouble in his life. The devil caused it. An interesting fact about Job is that he never got mad at God, even though he wrongfully thought God did these things to him.

My second favorite story of love is in the book of Ruth. In chapter 5, we see favor extended to Ruth. Ruth was not out looking for a man. After Naomi's husband died, she decided to leave Moab and return to Bethlehem, where she had family. She urged Ruth, her daughter-in-law, who was also a widow, to stay in Moab, where she might find another husband, but Ruth chose to stay with Naomi. So they came to Bethlehem to live. They were just trying to survive. As the barley harvest was just beginning, Ruth went into one of the fields to gather grain for herself and Naomi after the harvesters finished. It turned out that the field she began working in was owned by Boaz. He noticed her and went to talk with her. He suggested that she continue working in his field, which was probably safer than the others.

Boaz then instructed the harvesters to leave some extra grain for her to pick up. He also told them not to touch her. When Naomi saw the amount of grain Ruth brought home, she was delighted and asked who gave her such a favor. Ruth said that she had worked in the field of Boaz. Naomi told Ruth that Boaz was her relative on her husband's side. He was one of their kinsman-redeemers. A kinsman-redeemer was a male who was responsible for acting on behalf of a relative who was in need, trouble, or danger. Naomi was excited that his field was the one Ruth happened to be working in.

Naomi knew that the harvesters would be on the threshing floor and told Ruth to go there without Boaz knowing about it. When he was asleep, she was to uncover his feet and lie down. In the middle of the night, something startled him, and he saw that a woman was at his feet. He asked her name, and she told him. She also asked that he put the corner of his garment over her because he was a kinsman-redeemer. This action was a request for marriage. He explained to her that there was a closer relative who came first, but if he chose not to redeem her, Boaz would do it.

The closer relative declined, and Ruth and Boaz soon were married. They had a beautiful life together and had a child named Obed. He was the father of Jesse, the father of David.

Romance was quite different in those days. There were no places to take a date. We do not read about any restaurants or movie theaters. Life was very different in biblical times.

My daughter, Angie, in her early forties, had decided that she would be single for the rest of her life. She was at peace with that. She had plenty of friends, a job that she loved, and, of course, a dog. She also had a coffee cup that said, "Single all the way." I now have that cup! She wanted to go to a church where she could be involved in their various activities instead of just being in church every Sunday. She found the church to have great sermons, loving people, and lots of activity.

One Sunday, the pastor's wife, Nicole, who is also a close friend of Angie's, told her she wanted her to meet someone. She introduced Angie to Josh, a member of the church who had attended for over twenty years. Angie and her new acquaintance had lunch after church that day with Pastor Mike and Nicole. Their friendship blossomed into dating, and they were later married.

They included me on a few of their dates. How special is that? I was visiting with Josh in an ice cream parlor while Angie was visiting with some friends. I commented that Angie thought she was going to be single all her life. Josh's reply was that he, too, had felt that he would be single for the rest of his life. God knows how to bring people together.

The bridal shower at the church gave me a chance to meet some of Angie's church family. The guests took turns standing up and telling how they knew Josh or Angie. Most of the women who knew Josh shared that they had prayed for him for years that God would provide a wife for him. The women who knew Angie said the same about her. So many prayers had been sent on their behalf. This was the best part of the shower!

My favorite love story is about Jesus. John 3:16 (NLT) says, "For this is how God loved the world. He gave his one and only son so that everyone who believes in him will not perish but have eternal life." God did not send his son into the world to condemn it but to save it.

When I think about how he willingly allowed his body to be tortured, including stripes laid on his back, paying the price for mankind, I know that is love in its purest form. The Bible says that by his stripes, we were healed. He was sinless, yet he took our sin upon himself. Part of the torture was hanging on the cross. We cannot comprehend the depth of his love for us.

In the third chapter of 1 Kings, we see a judgment by King Solomon. Two mothers were claiming the same baby. With the information given, he was not able to determine which woman was the real mother. He called for a sword to be brought to him and declared his judgment: the baby would be cut in two, and each woman would receive half. One of the women asked that the king would give the baby to the other woman instead of killing him. The other woman said that the child should be cut in two. A mother's love showed the king who the real mother was. This story was an excellent display of Solomon's wisdom as well as the strength of a mother's love.

Many people grew up in a dysfunctional home. Love was not expressed nor taught in that home. Sometimes, children were told that they would never become successful in life. Those wounds are deep, and if they are not healed, they can affect a person's life in a negative way. It is hard to love yourself or someone else if love has not been shown to you.

The love of God, as shown in the scriptures, is hard for these people to comprehend because of the wounds. But if they keep pressing in, getting closer to God, they will find healing for those wounds. God knows everything about us and can help us fulfill our destiny. I still remember the times I spent before the Lord saying, "God, I want to be free." I knew I needed his help. I just did not know what kind of help I needed, but he knew. One of his names is El Shaddai, the one who is more than enough. He helped me so much that my request changed to this: "God, I want to help others to be free." He honored my request.

Tyson, my son, had a horse named Thunder. He loved that horse and took good care of him. But hard times came to us, and he was no longer able to keep him. It broke my heart that I was unable to help him in his time of need. Tyson took care of Thunder as long as he could and then reluctantly sold him at a horse auction. This was a traumatic time, as we knew that most auctioned horses end up at the slaughter plant.

Several years later, out of the blue, God gave me a message to give to Tyson. Although Tyson thought Thunder was gone forever, God had brought him to Tyson's ranch in heaven. Thunder was enjoying his time in heaven, and Tyson would one day be with him again. For us, messages like this are just an out-of-the-blue experience, but for God, it is perfect timing. Why did God choose this time in our lives to share this message? It brightened our day, and only God knows about the timing of the message. His ways are higher than ours, and his thoughts are higher than ours. God shows his love for us in ways that surprise us.

Love, according to the world, depends on circumstances. God loves us unconditionally. We cannot earn his love. Jesus was asked in Matthew 22 which of the Ten Commandments was the greatest. He replied that the first one was the greatest, which said, "Love the Lord your God with all your heart and with all your soul and with all your mind." Loving Him helps us to love others.

CHAPTER 13

Trust and Hope

God does not expect us to understand everything. He asks us to trust him. "Trust in the Lord with all your heart and lean not on your own understanding. In all your ways, acknowledge him, and he shall direct your path." (Prov. 3:5–6) We are not to use God as a last resort. He wants us to put him first and not to trust in ourselves. God is not only with us in the good times. He is also here in the struggles of life. Here is the definition of trust: firm belief in the reliability, truth, ability, or strength of someone or something. If our focus is more on God than the situation we are in, it shows that we are really trusting in him.

There is a clear picture of trust in the book of Judges. Deborah completely trusted God. He told her to command Barak, a general in the Lord's army, to go to battle against Sisera, the commander of the enemy army. She had no doubt that she heard from the Lord. Barak said he would do as she said, but only if she went with him. She accompanied him, and the Lord gave them the victory.

Shadrach, Meshach, and Abednego trusted God, even when they were thrown into the fiery furnace. They refused to serve the false gods, and they refused to worship the gold statue. God honored them, and they were not harmed at all by the fire. They did not even smell like smoke.

As the Israelites headed toward the Red Sea after leaving Egypt, Moses trusted God every step of the way. Because he did, the Israelites were able to cross the Red Sea on dry ground. If he had not trusted God and obeyed his commands, Pharoah's army would have overtaken them.

As I think about these situations and how God moved on their behalf, I am reminded of this verse: "Commit everything you do to the Lord. Trust him, and he will help you" (Ps. 37:5 NLT). This is one I need written on a sticky note so I can refer to it often. Things just go better when I get God involved in what I am doing. I have found that if my focus is more on God than the situation, it shows that is where my trust is.

This scripture is very comforting: "Whenever I am afraid, I will trust in you" (Ps. 56:3 NKJV). We are afraid at times. God invites us to come near to him. We cannot do anything about it, so let God into our situation. This scripture reinforces the fact that God wants to be an active part of our lives. Do not go to God last. Put him first. We know God isn't just with us in the good times. He is also here in our struggles.

Daniel's trust in God was so strong that he was not worried about being thrown into the lion's den. Daniel 6:23 (NLT) shows us the outcome: The king was overjoyed and ordered that Daniel be lifted from the den. Not a scratch was found on him, for he had trusted in his God.

The Lord told Gideon that he would use him to free Israel from the oppression of the Midianites. An angel appeared to him and called him a mighty warrior. Gideon's picture of himself was anything but a mighty warrior. He said he was the least in his family. He acted like God chose the wrong man for the job. God gave him some instructions, and he saw that God was serious about using him to win this battle. So, he accepted the challenge.

Gideon puts the word out that he needs help for the battle, and 32,000 men responded. The Lord told him that were too many. The count went down to 10,000. Again, the Lord said there is too many. The Midian army consisted of 135,000 men. It was obvious that they were greatly outnumbered. They finally ended up with 300 men for the battle. Remember that scripture that says with men, these things are impossible, but with God, all things are possible? An army of 300 ready to fight 135,000 looked very impossible. Gideon knew he needed to trust God more than ever now. The seventh chapter of Judges talks about the battle being won without their fighting. He chose to trust, and God honored him.

God does not want us to trust in ourselves. This is mentioned in Proverbs 11:28 (AMP): "He who leans on and trusts in and is confident in his riches will fall, but the righteous [who trust in God's provision] will flourish like a green leaf." We have a destiny to fulfill, and we need God's help every step of the way. His plans for us are far better than anything we can come up with.

An example of this is shown in the life of Joseph. Bad things kept happening to him, but he continued to trust God. He would see segments of victory in between the bad circumstances. In the end, he was second in charge of Egypt, with only Pharoah ahead of him. He could have been bitter and unforgiving, but instead, he chose to trust God. Many times during his life, it looked like the enemy was winning. This incredible story is found in chapter 41 of Genesis.

Isaiah 26 tells us that God will keep us in perfect peace as we trust in him. Trusting in him will keep our minds uncluttered from the matters at hand. Worry does not produce anything positive. We cannot change our circumstances by worrying about them. In our growing relationship with the Lord, we learn to cast our cares on the one who cares for us, according to 1 Peter 5:7.

Hope has been with us for a long time. As children, we got up in the morning, hoping that we would do well in school. We hoped our lunch would be good. We hoped that the naughty kids at school would leave us alone. Those naughty children are now called bullies.

Moving ahead into the high school years, my hopes changed a little. I hoped that the cute boy in my class would ask me for a date. I hoped I could find a fun job to earn some money. As a senior in high school, my hopes and dreams were simple. I was not interested in college. In a conversation with the high school counselor, I told him that the only reason I would go to college would be to find a husband, and I knew that was wrong. So my hope was to find a great job using my office skills and to have a family of my own.

God has hopes for us. "For I know the plans I have for you, says the Lord. They are plans for good and not for evil, to give you a future and a hope" (Jeremiah 29:11 NLT). In Romans 15:13, we find even more encouragement. The New Living Translation says, "I pray that God, the source of hope, will fill you completely with joy and peace because you trust in him. Then you will overflow with confident hope through the power of the Holy Spirit."

The world teaches us to hope in money, determination, our own abilities, and luck. Several years ago, I worked at a grocery store. A man came in almost every day to buy lottery tickets. He believed in luck and hoped that he would soon win the lottery. My hope was that he would use that money to buy himself something good for dinner. The odds of winning the lottery are not very good. Every day, we choose where to look for hope, in the things around us or in the Creator. God has a destiny for each of us, and it is his hope that we seek his ways and not the ways of the world. We are reminded in Isaiah 55 that his thoughts are higher than ours, and his ways are higher than ours. So our goal should be for the best that God has for us, not just barely getting by.

One of the biggest lies the devil tells us is that God does not have time for us and that our hopes and dreams are not important to him. The truth is that he is our loving heavenly Father, and we are his children. He delights in spending time with us and encourages us to come to him even in the smallest things. He wants a relationship with us. How can we have a relationship with someone if we ignore them all the time? We cannot get to know someone if we are not willing to spend time with them. The time we spend in God's presence is valuable. We get to know him as we fellowship with him. If we have become Christians, the Holy Spirit is with us all the time. We should acknowledge him! Several years ago, Benny Hinn wrote a book called "Good Morning Holy Spirit." He had such a strong relationship with the Holy Spirit that he wrote a book about it!

There are areas where we need more understanding, and our hope is that God will give us revelation so we can make better decisions. Life is not always easy, but our hope should be in God, who knows all things. The more we hope for the future, the less our thoughts are stuck in the past.

Hope sends a beam of sunshine into that darkness we are experiencing. In Hebrews 11, we are shown that faith and hope work together. Psalm 147:11 is very encouraging. It says that the Lord delights in those who fear him, those who put their hope in his unfailing love.

When you are in despair, you need hope more than ever. When you are too down in the dumps to know what to ask God for, ask him for hope. Ask him for help. I often prayed Psalm 50:15 (NLT) when I was going through difficult circumstances. "Trust me in your times of trouble, and I will rescue you, and you will give me glory." The help I received from the Lord started out with his showing me a different perspective of what I was dealing with. He showed me his thoughts on the matter. He helped me so much that I kept that scripture handy.

Hope is practical. We do not just sit and wait for our situations to improve. Hope motivates us to get up and do something instead of sinking in despair. It helps us to get our minds on positive things if we choose to cooperate with the Lord's leading. We do not know the future, but God does. So since we have no control over the future, we hope in God, who has charge of the future. "For in you, O Lord, I hope; you will answer, O Lord my God" (Psalms 38:15 AMP).

Hope does not disappoint. It is a positive thing. In Romans 5, we are encouraged in this. More encouragement comes in Psalm 33:18 (NIV): In Isaiah 40, we are shown that those who hope in the Lord will renew their strength. The Lord shows us scripture after scripture, reinforcing the fact that he wants us to make it. He wants us to have a good life.

As I read this next psalm written by David, I am reminded of the intense hardships he encountered in his life and his unfailing love for God. Psalm 71:14 (NLT): "But I will keep on hoping for you to help me. I will praise you more and more." God gives us the courage to keep hoping, even when we feel like giving up.

While writing this chapter, a quick thought about Jonah made me laugh. His three days and nights in the belly of the big fish probably stirred up some hope during that terrifying time. I am sure he hoped God would hear his prayer and rescue him. As we look at the people written in the Bible, we see hope arise in their difficult circumstances. Hope is there, but we do not always notice it.

Abraham did not just hope. He hoped against hope, according to Romans 4:18. This means holding on even when the odds are against you. He was a hundred years old when God promised that he would be the father of many nations. That looked impossible. He hoped in the promise instead of what he saw in the natural. Romans 8:25 (NLT) says, "If we look forward to something we do not have yet, we must wait patiently and confidently." It took a long time for the blessing he was promised. Many of us would have given up hope, thinking that we really did not hear from God. But Abraham's relationship with God was strong. He knew he had heard from God.

What about false hope? The dictionary describes false hope as confident feelings about something that might not be true. Hoping to win the lottery falls into this category.

I want God to keep watch over me. Psalm 33:18 says that the eyes of the Lord are on those who fear him, on those whose hope is in his unfailing love. He has my back, and I am thankful for that.

Faith and hope work together, as we are shown in Hebrews 11. It says that faith is the confident assurance that what we hope for is going to happen. We are encouraged to put our hope in the Lord in Psalm 33. If our hope and trust are only in material things, they will, at some point, bring disappointment. We have a destiny from the Lord, and it is better than anything we can produce.

Jesus is the same yesterday, today, and forever, according to Hebrews 13:8. Those wonderful things he did in the Bible are still available today. He never quit healing and delivering. The Bible stories are not just a history lesson. They show us that help is also available to us. What he did for them, he will do for us. He wants us to fulfill our destiny. Let him be a part of your life. He is just a prayer away.

CHAPTER 14

Our Covenant with God

By accepting Jesus as our Savior, we entered a covenant with God, which was bought and paid for by the blood of Jesus. Because of that covenant, we now have rights and privileges that were not previously available to us. All Bible promises are covenant promises.

A famous covenant is in Genesis 9:11, where God promises he will never flood the earth again. In this covenant, he gave a symbol of his promise, which is the rainbow.

In the old covenant, sin had to be taken care of by animal sacrifices once a year. This made atonement for all the sins. In the new covenant, the focus is on what God has done for us in Jesus. Atonement was taken care of forever, not yearly.

In part of 1 Corinthians 11:24 and 25 (NLT), look what the Bible says about Jesus in the upper room with the disciples: He gave thanks to God, broke the bread in pieces, and said, "This is my body, which is given for you. Do this in remembrance of me." He took the cup of wine after supper, saying, "This cup is the new covenant between God and his people—an agreement confirmed with my blood. Do this in remembrance of me as often as you drink it."

Whenever we take communion, it is a celebration of our covenant with God, which was bought and paid for by the blood of Jesus.

Jesus willingly went to the cross for us. He bore thirty-nine stripes, and his blood was poured out for us so we could be forgiven of our sins and our bodies could be healed. When he did this, he was establishing the new covenant.

Many know about what Jesus did for us but are not aware that we have a covenant because of his sacrifice. Our lack of awareness keeps us from placing a demand on what belongs to us. God wants us to enjoy the benefit of his promises to us, but we need to claim them. How do we claim them? Throughout the Bible, God is encouraging his people to come to him and ask him for what they need. Our salvation began with prayer, and so will our needs. There are many scriptures for this, but one of my favorites is Psalm 34:17 (NLT): "The Lord hears his people when they call to him for help. He rescues them from all their troubles."

Our God keeps his covenant promises. His unfailing love is shown throughout the Bible in the many covenants he made with his people.

If you are not yet a born-again Christian, you may be wondering what it says about that in the Bible.

Jesus replied,

> I assure you; no one can enter the Kingdom of God without being born of water and the Spirit. Humans can reproduce only human life, but the Holy Spirit gives birth to spiritual life. So don't be surprised when I say, "You must be born again." (John 3:5–7 NLT)

Romans 10:9–10 says that if you declare with your mouth that Jesus is Lord and believe in your heart that God raised him from the dead, you will be saved. For it is with your heart that you believe and are justified, and it is with your mouth that you profess your faith and are saved.

To receive Jesus Christ as your Lord and Savior of your life, sincerely pray this prayer out loud from your heart:

> Dear Jesus, I believe that you died and rose again on the third day. I confess to you that I am

a sinner, and I need your forgiveness and your love. Come into my life, forgive my sins, and give me eternal life. I confess you now as my Lord and Savior. Thank you for my salvation. Amen.

God gives us choices all the time. We can choose to do right or wrong. We make choices all day long. God has given each of us a destiny. No one was left out. He loves us all the same. Look what the scripture says about us in Jeremiah 29:11 (NIV): "For I know the plans I have for you," declares the Lord, "plans to prosper you and not to harm you, plans to give you hope and a future." This is better than anything we could ever plan!

The first part of James 4:8 (NKJV) says, "Draw near to God and he will draw near to you." That is an easy invitation. Our heavenly Father loves us so much. He knows what will bless us, and He knows what will hurt us. He has our back, but he wants our cooperation. So let us look at our life as an adventure with God, looking forward to what he has in store for us. In my first book, Get Real with God, I made this statement: "Life is a journey. Enjoy the ride." I am enjoying the ride, and I hope the same is true for you.

CHAPTER 15

Beauty for Ashes
My Testimony

Part of Mark 10:9 (NIV) says, "What God has joined together, let no one separate." This beautiful scripture was part of my marriage ceremony. It took me thirty-six years to realize that God is not in every marriage.

Nine years into my marriage, I asked Jesus to be my Lord and Savior. With that born-again experience came a strong desire to pray. That desire never left.

One of the things on my prayer list was for the healing of my marriage. Abuse was a part of my life, and I told my husband that if he ever hit me, it would be the end of our marriage. Abuse comes in different packages. One day, I suggested that we go to a marriage counselor. His response was "Why? It's all your fault."

My husband was a mail carrier in a town of 1,500. Every day, people saw this friendly, helpful man who worked with the public. Some of his personal time was spent drinking coffee with friends at the local convenience store or riding his motorcycle. Many people thought we were a happy couple. What they did not see was what went on behind closed doors.

In developing a relationship with Jesus, I asked him to help me in my marriage. I felt that, somehow, I was triggering the abusive behavior of my husband. I asked Jesus to help me to be a better person and a better wife so that I would not cause the outbursts of rage against me.

Some Christian friends offered advice in my journey to victory. Some suggested to keep praying because God is faithful. Others commented that God does not expect us to remain in an abusive environment. At this time, I did not feel strong enough to go through with a divorce, so I continued to pray for the healing of my marriage. What I discovered was that one person cannot heal a marriage. Both parties need to be involved. As I look back, I see that I would have stayed in a loveless marriage. Part of the marriage vows says, "For better or for worse."

The strong desire to pray was a blessing from God. It caused me to spend a lot of one-on-one time with him. This time with him gave me the strength to walk away from the marriage when the time was right.

During the last year with my husband, I prayed that the Lord would cause him to fall asleep as soon as he went to bed so that I could have a peaceful night. God honored my request.

My coworkers had no idea what my personal life was like. I loved my job and did it well. I put on a smile at work, although the real me was a mess.

During the last week of my marriage, I was up in the middle of the night vomiting because of a recurring nightmare. The night before I left my husband, I was unable to sleep. I spent this time before the Lord with one scripture he gave me to meditate on, Philippians 4:13 (NKJV): "I can do all things through Christ who strengthens me." This one-on-one time with the Lord was exactly what I needed.

It was almost time to get up and get ready for work. I was directed to get up, turn off the alarm, write a note to my husband, leave it on the kitchen table, and go to work. In the natural, I would not have had the strength or the courage to do what I needed to do.

My very surprised husband read the note when he got up. By the grace of God, we went our separate ways. There was no fighting over the division of our possessions, and we used the same lawyer to save money. I believe he was relieved that it was finally over.

I planned on getting an apartment, but our daughter insisted that I move in with her. Her friends became my friends, and the healing process began.

God's Word came to my rescue during my tumultuous marriage. He sent me a scripture as I needed it. I accepted his help and prayed his Word into my circumstances, knowing that somehow, God always wins.

At the age of sixty-one, I started my life over. I forgave my husband and prayed for his salvation. Some would think this was a hard choice at my age, but I was not afraid to start over. I was grateful to be away from an abusive life. Peace is sweet.

Part of 1 Corinthians 2:9 says, "No eye has seen, no ear has heard, and no mind has imagined what God has prepared for those who love him." He gave me beauty for ashes, as said in Isaiah 61:3.

My heart is now happy, and I am forever grateful to the one who created me. He is also the one who knew how to fix me. In my first book, *Get Real with God*, I made this statement: "Life is a journey. Enjoy the ride." My journey has been one adventure after another, and, yes, I am now enjoying the ride.

ABOUT THE AUTHOR

Several people have asked what motivated me to write my books. The best answer would be obedience to the Lord. As I was sitting in my living room about bedtime, Jesus appeared and said one sentence to me: "I want you to write a book." I sat in silence for a moment, not knowing what to say. I saw myself as someone who prays for people. I did not think anyone would be interested in anything I had to say. Then he said, "The name of your book will be Get Real with God." This changed the atmosphere, and I now thought I must have something to say to people because Jesus thinks I do. My response was simply, "Okay."

Shortly thereafter, I would be awakened in the night with a few paragraphs for my new book. I got up and wrote what I saw and then returned to bed. A few hours later, more paragraphs came forth. Again, I got up and wrote a few more paragraphs, thinking I had not thought of these things in a long time. When the alarm rang in the morning, I was surprised that I felt like I had a good night's sleep.

Later, the Lord again spoke to me, saying, "The title of your next book is *Progressive Healing.*"

I was amused by this new chapter in my life and said, "Hmmm, I must be an author!"

I seek the Lord's direction as I am writing the books. I never would have guessed that this is part of my destiny. As I said in my first book, "Life is a journey. Enjoy the ride." This part of my journey is fun. I am enjoying it.

The Lord gave me the title of this book as well as the first two. A lot of time was spent before Him during the writing of this book because I really did not know what to write. It was exciting to see it come together.

I work full-time at a nursing home and teach Bible study for them three times a week. My favorite activities are dining out with friends, going to movies, especially comedies, playing dominoes, and putting jigsaw puzzles together. I also love oil painting but have not had the time to invest in that lately.

This book is not a substitute for professional medical treatment or advice. This book is only a resource for encouragement and prayer.

Your feedback is welcomed, and you may write to me at this email address: dorothykuehn2017@outlook.com

www.ingramcontent.com/pod-product-compliance
Lightning Source LLC
Chambersburg PA
CBHW021123130726
47988CB00003B/1135